The Goat Handbook

Ulrich Jaudas and Seyedmehdi Mobini, DVM

Full-color Photographs
Illustrations by Fritz W. Köhler

About the Authors

Dr. Jaudas, a professor at Hohenheim University in Germany, has been an agricultural advisor in Africa and has many years of experience with goats. Dr. Mobini, a professor of veterinary science at Fort Valley State University, has 28 years of experience as a veterinarian and an educator. He has published numerous articles on the health and breeding of goats in scientific journals. *The Goat Handbook* is their first book for Barron's.

Photo Credits

Norvia Behling: 9, 28, 36, 86, 105, 106, 117, 119, 120, and 123; Gerry Bucsis and Barbara Somerville: viii, 4, 5, 7, 8, 11, 12, 18, 25, 27, 32, 33, 45, 51, 53, 55, 56, 63, 64, 65, 70, 77, 78, 85, 92, 110, 111, 125, 126, 128 (top and bottom left), 129 (bottom), and 133; Coleman/Burton: vii (top left, top right, and bottom right); Coleman/Reinhard: vi; Ecke: 61; Seyedmehdi Mobini: 14, 17, 19, 22, 24, 30, 41, 52, 54, 58, 60, 67, 72, 79, 81, 84, 127, 128 (bottom right), and 130 (top and bottom); Reinhard: vii (bottom left), 23, 31, and 131 (top, middle, and bottom); Silvestris/Eckhardt: 59; Skogstad: 39, 95 (top left, top right, center left, center right, bottom left, and bottom right), 99, 100, and 129 (top); and Connie Summers: 20, 35, and 122.

Cover Photos

Norvia Behling: inside front cover and inside back cover and Gerry Bucsis and Barbara Somerville: front cover and back cover.

Copyright © 1987 by Gräfe and Unzer GmbH, Munich.
Title of the German original: *Ziegen*.

All inquiries should be addressed to:
Barron's Educational Series, Inc.
250 Wireless Boulevard
Hauppauge, New York 11788
www.barronseduc.com

Library of Congress Catalog Card No. 2005050022

ISBN-13: 978-0-7641-3268-1
ISBN-10: 0-7641-3268-7

Library of Congress Cataloging-in-Publication Data
Mobini, Seyedmehdi.
　　The goat handbook / Seyedmehdi Mobini and Ulrich Jaudas.
　　　　p. cm.
　　Previously published in German as: Ziegen.
　　Rev. ed. of: The new goat handbook. / Ulrich Jaudas. c1989.
　　Includes bibliographical references (p.) and index.
　　ISBN 0-7641-3268-7 (alk. paper)
　　1. Goats. I. Jaudas, Ulrich, 1948– New goat handbook. II. Title.

SF383.J3813　2006
636.3′9—dc22　　　　　　　　　　　　2005050022

Printed in China
9 8 7 6 5

Important Note

This handbook tells the reader how to buy and care for goats. The authors and publisher consider it important to point out that the advice given in this book is meant primarily for normally developed goats of excellent physical health and good character.

Anyone who adopts a fully grown goat should be aware that the animal has already formed its basic impressions of human beings. The new owner should watch the animal carefully, including its behavior toward humans, and should meet the previous owner.

Caution is further advised in the association of children with goats and in exercising goats without proper safeguards.

Even well-behaved and carefully supervised goats sometimes do damage to someone else's property or cause accidents. It is therefore in the owner's interest to be adequately insured against such eventualities, and we strongly urge all goat owners to purchase a liability policy that covers their goat(s).

Goat farmers who wish to sell goat products must comply with local food protection regulations. Because these vary from area to area, goat keepers should obtain information from the local authorities.

Contents

Preface

More and more people today want their food to be natural and when shopping will gladly go to considerable trouble to see that it is. Under these circumstances, goat keeping is once more becoming important. But today who still knows the right way to keep goats? Many questions that arise for the beginner, and also often for the experienced goat keeper, are discussed and provided with expert answers in this manual. The authors, Seyedmehdi Mobini and Ulrich Jaudas, are college professors; an important part of their research and teaching is the study of goat husbandry. They have wide practical experience—for years

This Dwarf feeds its kid.

they have been successfully keeping and raising goats. In this book they share their knowledge and experience. Advice on buying helps you choose the right goat breed. The authors describe in detail which breeds are suitable for milk and which are suitable for meat production. They also tell you about the breeds with hair (laypeople often say wool) that can be utilized. And of course they do not omit discussion of the popular dwarf goats, which are often kept for the pleasure of having animals to take care of, because they develop into devoted pets.

Every goat keeper should know about correct housing of goats. The precise directions and the informative drawings in this book give you extensive information about suitable stabling and furnishings as well as about keeping goats in a pasture.

Proper feed is important for the cud-chewing goat. Therefore the authors go into detail about digestion, nutrients, various types of fodder, their production, and how to feed. Goats do eat plants that sheep and cattle will not, to be sure, but at the same time they are very choosy. For many a self-sustaining farmer it is an

An Alpine goat grazing in the field.

A Golden Guernsey walking in a field.

This Russian Don is chewing on some hay.

Three Nubians survey their surroundings.

advantage that goats can be easily kept with other grazing animals just because of their special eating behavior and their food preferences.

How you keep your goats healthy and what you yourself can do for the prevention and treatment of sickness in the animals is described in detail in the chapter Healthy Maintenance and Sickness.

You will receive expert and comprehensive advice about breeding and raising goats, because goats give milk only when they have born kids. A special chapter focuses on the products of goats. In it, you will find information that is indispensable if you want to become self-sufficient: information about milk production, milking, and the making of sour milk, yogurt, cheese, and butter, and advice on obtaining meat.

The chapter Goat Breeds of the World tells how domestic goats are kept all over the world and what goat breeds there are.

The authors and publisher thank all who have collaborated on this book, especially Fritz W. Köhler for the informative drawings.

Chapter One

The Nature of the Goat

The Goat in Myth and Fairy Tale

In general, the role of the goat in literature is that of the stubborn seeker of heights. We need only think of Alphonse Daudet's "The Goat of Monsieur Seguin," who does not allow herself to be dissuaded from her decision, even though she expects to be eaten by the wolf.

An extraordinary number of myths have collected around the goat. The Old Testament describes the "scapegoat," on which all sins are loaded and which is then driven out into the desert with this burden. Since ancient times the goat—and most especially the he-goat—has been associated with supernatural powers. Goats of a godly nature—especially as fertility gods—or of a devilish one have both been common. The Greek deity of the forest and flocks, Pan, was born in the form of a goat; he was valued as the benefactor of fertility of the flocks and the wild animals.

The Teutons believed that two he-goats pulled the chariot of Thor when

This Alpine doe is resting in a field.

he drove through the heavens in a storm with peals of thunder. When it hails, people in southern Germany today sometimes still speak of "kids' onions"; without realizing it, they are talking about the droppings that fell from Thor's goats. And finally, in Christian mythology, the devil is represented in the form of a goat.

The Special Nature of the Goat

In truth it is not only in fairy tales and myths that the nature of the goat invites special attention. Its peculiarities are noteworthy, and you should actually see one with your own eyes before you acquire such an animal.

To human beings the goat seems uncommonly curious. It observes strange circumstances and people alertly. In danger it proves to be courageous; many a dog has great respect for goats, having made the unpleasant acquaintance of its horns. Goats are able to assess novel situations surprisingly quickly and to use them to their advantage.

Daring climbers and jumpers, they can overcome rock barriers as well as the walls of box stalls and prefer to get to a high place where they can observe their surroundings.

Although every goat, even within a herd, goes its own way, it is nevertheless very sociable and is not happy as a loner. Within the herd there is a firm ranking order in which a lead doe and a lead buck share the duties of leader. If there is no male, this role usually falls to the goats' keeper. When new goats come into a herd, or goats from one stock are joined to another group, the ranking order is established by dueling. The rivals fight, forehead against forehead, and very seldom is either one injured. On the other hand, goats attack enemies, such as dogs, in tender spots with the tips of their horns.

The Capricious Goat

The goat has an inexhaustible capacity for the kind of behavior that seems to the goat keeper either to be silly or to result in malicious pranks. Goats can also be very obstinate if they get an idea into their heads or don't want to do something that the goat keeper would like done. This peculiarity has even gotten into the language. The Latin name of goats, *capra*, is contained in the word *capricious*, which describes their elegant movements as well as their moody and unpredictable behavior. *Capers* denotes the exuberant little jumps of the kids, but also the unexpected sallies even of sedate mother goats.

The goat keeper must adjust to goats' singular behavior and outwit them if necessary. Out-and-out coercive measures are seldom successful. Then, goats mostly resort to passive resistance, in which they will no longer move from the spot and may even refuse to eat.

Their eating behavior also seems capricious. Goats are markedly choosy and seek only the tastiest morsels in the pasture or from the feed offered them. Thus it often happens that in the middle of the finest meadow they want a piece of paper on the other side of the fence or the string of an apron on the clothesline.

Goat Language

Everyone knows that bleating is the language of goats, and it is not by chance that this concept is also used in a figurative sense. For, in fact, there is scarcely anything more irksome than the constant and reproachful-sounding bleating of a goat that is standing in front of a filled feed trough and has decided it wants something else.

As goat keeper you will soon find out that there are many variations in bleating and will learn to understand their meanings. There is the joyful bleating with which the goat greets you when you enter the stable, the bleating with which the mother coaxes her kid, or the bleating of the doe in heat, which can be heard far and wide.

There are other sounds besides-for example, the *huhu* with which the buck woos the doe, or a rattling noise through the nose that serves as a warning to the herd or, if necessary, also as a signal for flight. When in great pain, the goat complains with a groan.

The Difference from Sheep

Goats are related to sheep, but crossing, as a rule, is not possible. Attempts at mating sheep and goats are certainly not rare, and occasionally a crossbreed may even result. Such histories may be the reason that there are breeds of sheep and goats that appear very similar to each other.

Among the European and American breeds, sheep and goats are usually easy to tell apart, mainly because of the wool of the sheep. With the short-haired sheep breeds that are usually found in the tropics, this is somewhat more difficult because the body build of sheep and goat does not exhibit any basic differences that are immediately apparent to the naked eye. In the skeleton there are a few minor but definite differences that have permitted the classification of archeological finds. In living animals it is primarily behavior that characterizes the difference between sheep and goats.

Behavior

In the pasture, sheep maintain a herd, at least loosely, whereas goats spread out and look for food individually. Goats can stand on their hind legs to reach bushes and trees so that they can eat the leaves they particularly like, whereas sheep are not able to do this and prefer grass and weeds. Strange circumstances and people are observed very carefully by goats. Although they remove themselves with a few jumps when danger threatens, they do it only so they can better observe the threat. Sheep, on the other hand, are easily panicked and then the whole herd storms away. It is enough if one animal takes off in flight; the others will follow it blindly. For this reason, goat bucks are used as lead animals for sheep herds.

When they duel, two goat bucks stand on their hind legs so as to drive their heads together when they drop, whereas rams clash their heads together horizontally with a lightning-swift attack, like a battering ram. The gait of the goat appears graceful, whereas the sheep has a pronounced waddle when walking. An especially good mark of difference is the carriage of the tail. Sheep let it hang; goats carry it upright.

Chapter Two

Considerations Before Buying

If you are thinking of keeping goats, it's helpful to clarify beforehand not only what you expect of the goats but also what you can offer them and what you are prepared to do for them.

A Goat as a Pet or as a Useful Animal

If you are looking for animals to keep your lawn trimmed, you won't be happy with goats because of the way they graze. In this case, sheep are much better "lawn mowers."

Pets

If you want goats for the fun of working with animals but are not looking for any material profit, dwarf goats can provide you with much pleasure. Of course, dwarf goats can also contribute meat if you want to be self-supporting, and they provide manure for the garden, in any case.

Milk Production

If the aim of goat keeping is to provide self-support with milk or even the sale of milk and milk prod-

ucts, naturally the milk breeds such as the white and the colored *Saanen* are most suitable. Kids for slaughter are then a by-product.

Bear in mind, however, that milk goats require not only more work for milking but also regular attention as well. Except for the short period of dryness at the end of pregnancy, they must be milked twice daily, even on weekends and when you are on vacation. Neglect or irregularities in feeding can quickly lead to health problems in milk goats.

Meat Production

If you cannot or do not wish to undertake the labor of keeping milk goats but nevertheless want a return from your goat keeping, either for your own use or for market, you should decide on meat goats. Of course you will then have no milk, since there will be only enough for raising the kids. If someone will keep an eye on the goats, you may even go on vacation without worrying.

Fiber Production

If you enjoy working with wool, you might try keeping angora goats.

The Angora goat is kept for fiber production.

What You Must Offer

Work Expenditure and Food Supply

Besides the amount of work that you can do or want to do, you must examine what you have available for a food supply. How many meadows and fields do you own or can you perhaps lease? Where can you buy feed and at what price? Must you build fences? What must you spend for them?

Permissibility

If you live in a thickly settled area, you should find out ahead of time whether keeping goats is permitted. And even if there are no legal restrictions on keeping goats, it is still always wise to be on good terms with the neighbors with regard to the goats. Not infrequently the joyous

bleating of the goats is experienced by an annoyed neighbor as disturbing noise. Offering a freshly made goat cheese over the fence every now and again can help to guard against such annoyance.

Bucks

Still to be clarified is where the nearest buck is available for mating. With a pickup truck, even a trip to the buck is not a problem, and since goats normally mate only once a year, the trouble required for a small herd is inconsequential.

Keeping Single Animals

You should know, too, that goats are not happy when kept singly. Of course, if a goat comes to you as a kid, and you can take care of it regularly and play with it within the compass of its natural behavior, then to

A small herd of goats congregating together in an enclosed pen.

some degree you can take the place of its companions in a herd. Other pets may also assume this role, although innate behavior sets limits. Large dogs, for instance, are frequently attacked by mother goats. Obviously, the conflict of wild goats with wolves has left behind an inherited image of an enemy in our domestic goats.

Demands

If you buy a milk goat, you can of course begin to be self-sufficient right away, but at the same time you must fulfill the goat's high demands. On the other hand, if you start by buying a pregnant young doe or a not-yet-mated kid, you naturally have to wait a while to see the first return, but in exchange you have a chance to get to know your goat and its character.

Reasons for Keeping Goats

The goat supplies milk and meat. In addition, the production of leather and hair is important. Furthermore, the dung serves as fertilizer. In the Himalayas the goats are even used as beasts of burden. In Europe in earlier days it was not uncommon to see castrated bucks, for instance, hitched to a milk wagon. Even today there are occasional goat raisers who have made the harnessing of goats into a much-admired hobby.

Goats, therefore, contribute both to self-maintenance and to income.

This black-and-white Pygmy goat surveys the surroundings in a barnyard.

These functions can be fulfilled in the same way by other farm animals, but there are still some specific arguments for the keeping of goats.

• Compared to cattle, the goat is small. Thus not only is the cost of purchase reasonable, but goats can also be maintained with less feed. If several goats are kept instead of a cow, enough milk and meat may be produced for the needs of a family.

• In case of contagious disease, it is less likely that all goats in one family will perish. With the surviving goats, a new herd can be built up quickly, since twin and triple births are not uncommon with goats.

• The characteristic taste of goat's milk is especially popular in cheese, and the low-fat meat, especially that of the kid, is considered a delicacy everywhere.

• Because of their feed preferences and their feeding behavior, goats are frequently kept along with other grazing animals. They use the plants that are avoided by the others and at the same time also weed the field. Bushy meadows and steep mountain meadows are best used by goats.

Still, these same special eating habits of goats can also set limits to their keeping. Although, despite widely held opinion, goats are not to blame for large-scale destruction of vegetation—in the Sahara region, for example—goats can, when uncontrolled, wreak considerable damage in gardens, cultivated fields, and tree plantings.

The Goat—Ideal Animal for Self-sufficiency

Alienation from Nature

In our specialized industrialized society there are few people who actually see where their food comes from. Stores and the food industry stand between the user and the farmer and gardener, who also more and more are turning to the use of industrial production procedures. The conserving, harmonious dealing with earth, plants, and animals is being pushed aside by economic pressures; food is becoming loaded with pollutants—to some degree, pollutants from the processes of production itself, but primarily those from industry and heavy traffic. Many people are afraid that their food no longer meets their standards and thus consider raising it themselves.

Very few in our society can become completely independent, subsisting entirely on their own produce. But we are able to create a limited area in which we consciously experience how, with adroit collaboration with plants and animals, food is produced without harming nature. Goat husbandry, with its many demands but also with its multiple advantages, can be ideal for such an area.

Back to Nature with the Goat

The goat has always been of great importance as a source of independent provisioning for the family. With a few goats or even a single animal, the family's requirements for milk and meat are already provided for. After the birth of their young, goats give milk for almost a year. If the goat is not bred again, it can even be milked for up to two years without interruption. By postponing the dates of mating for eight to twelve weeks, one can guarantee regular milk production over a whole year in a herd of at least two goats.

Goat's milk may be drunk fresh, but it is also suited to the various processes for making sour milk, yogurt, cheese, and butter. If you keep your own goats, you will know the origin of all the foodstuffs these produce and can yourself ensure that they are of the best quality.

Goat keeping is the ideal complement for organic gardening. For one thing, you need add no further fertilizers to goat manure, and, for another, the plants used for crop rotation that do not produce direct yield, such as clover, serve as valuable feed. Much garden debris is suitable for feed.

Goats also graze small open spaces or edges of roads. If the feed must be used in a stable, transporting it is no problem because of the small amounts needed.

The economics of production are not the primary consideration for self-sufficient farmers. Therefore, they look for more than material profit in their domestic animals and take particular pleasure in the cheerful nature of the goat.

In order to have profit and pleasure from a goat, the keeper must satisfy its special demands for maintenance and feeding. Goats tolerate mistakes in these matters less well than many other domestic animals.

Chapter Three

Buying Goats

Now that you've clarified your particular purpose in getting a goat, it is important that you find the proper animal to fulfill it.

The Right Goat for Every Purpose

For Milk Production

The white and the colored Saanen are both highly recommended, since they have been bred for high milk production.

The *white Saanen* today can be expected to produce a milk yield of from 1,984 to 2,204 pounds (900 to 1,000 kg) per year, with a fat content of 3.6 percent and an albumin content of 2.7 percent. But high yields of over 3,968 pounds (1,800 kg) of milk per year have also been reported.

An adult white Saanen weighs about 132 pounds (60 kg); the buck is somewhat heavier than the female, weighing up to 198 pounds (90 kg). The height of the withers in the does is about 27 to 31 inches (70 to 80 cm), and in the bucks about 31 to 35 inches (80 to 90 cm).

The coat is predominantly short, smooth, and pure white. Frequently, there is a soft reddish or yellowish color on the back and neck, and the hair may be longer on the neck, back, and thighs.

The *colored Saanen* is predominantly brown and usually has a black eel stripe on the back. It is somewhat smaller and more delicate in structure than the white Saanen and gives a very slightly smaller quantity of milk.

Thus when choosing between white or colored Saanen goats, you can decide according to your preference for a certain color without being concerned about which is the better producer. The colored goats are considered less demanding and are better suited for high altitudes. White goats can suffer from sunburn if they are kept in pastures.

For Meat Production

If you keep milk goats there is also a considerable meat yield, since you can slaughter the kids that you don't need for further breeding. There are only a few goat breeds that are specifically raised for meat.

One of the authors spending some "quality time" with his white Saanens.

The *Boer* is one of these. Castrated bucks can weigh up to 220 pounds (100 kg). The coloration of the animals varies widely, but breeders strive for white with a red-brown neck and head. Further distinguishing marks are the hanging ears.

Boer goats have spread quickly in the last few years, especially among goat keepers who are interested in the kids for sale or slaughter, of course, but also to avoid the work involved in milking.

Since it was difficult to get breeding animals from South Africa because of veterinary restrictions, the few purebred Boer goats were mainly used for crossing with colored or white Saanen goats. The offspring are then crossed again with Boer goats. These repeated crossings have developed the modern meat goat, as the breed is officially designated, though popularly it is generally still called the Boer goat. Ample supply of purebred Boer goats are now available worldwide.

Another breed specifically raised for meat is the *Kiko* goat, which was developed in New Zealand. The Kiko is large framed, generally white. The Kiko is a consummate grazer with a good rate of growth.

For Fiber Production

The *Angora* is kept for the production of hair. This medium-sized goat has a pure-white curly coat that is shorn for the production of mohair. The goat originates in the Anatolian highlands of Turkey, and its name is derived from the city of Ankara.

Outside of Turkey, Angora goats today are raised primarily in South Africa and Texas. Attempts at breeding Angora goats are being made in England, France, and also in Germany, but the procurement of breeding animals from the traditional breeding areas is either difficult or impossible because of animal import restrictions, so that as yet only few breeding animals are obtainable.

As a Hobby

Dwarf varieties, which stem from Africa, have only a very small milk production, and their meat yield is also less than that of other breeds. Accordingly, their requirements for feed and housing space are also less, making them especially suitable if you just want to keep goats for the pleasure of dealing with animals.

There are dwarf goats in all possible color combinations; piebald animals are common.

Dwarf goats reproduce very rapidly, since because of their tropical origins they can be bred successfully at any time of year and since they frequently bear triplets.

Horned and Unhorned Goats

Horns are found in female as well as male goats, as is the beard. Nevertheless, hornless goats appear frequently, and in the breeding of certain breeds—for example, the colored and the white *Saanen*—these animals are chosen purposely. However, hornlessness brings with it certain important consequences.

Infertility

The gene for hornlessness is linked with a gene for the development of hermaphroditism. Female goats that are homozygously hornless have stunted interior sex organs and are barren. Externally they appear hermaphroditic, displaying an enlarged penislike clitoris or resembling a buck entirely. Homozygously hornless bucks can be potent, to be sure, but frequently they suffer from blocked semen. On the other hand, heterozygous hornless goats, which also carry a recessive gene for horns, and all horned goats are unrestrictedly fertile. If these are bred exclusively with hornless goats, an average of 25 to 50 percent of the offspring will be hermaphrodites and cannot be bred further.

Advantages and Disadvantages

In many goat herds the horned and unhorned goats live together without any trouble. In this situation, however, the horned animals absolutely must not be the dominant ones in the herd. The horns even of bucks offer no danger if one is careful moving around. Woundings of humans occur very seldom, and when they do, they are not ordinarily the result of an attack but occur because of human carelessness. Of course the animals can damage fences, hayracks, and so forth, but on the other hand they are very adept at scratching the various parts of their bodies with the tips of their horns.

If you cannot be persuaded to forego hornlessness, you should at least cover your goats with a horned

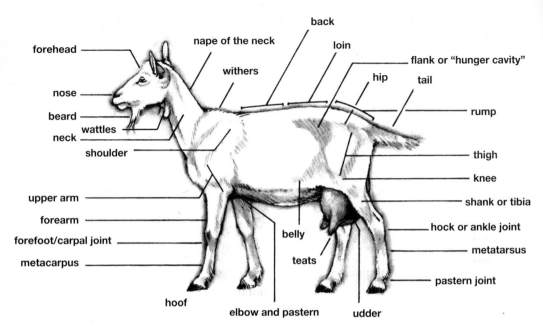

The anatomy of a typical goat. In order to take care of goats, one must be familiar with their different body parts.

buck. Then all the offspring, even the hornless ones, will be normally fertile.

Dehorning

To avoid the disadvantages of hermaphroditism but have hornless goats nonetheless, goats are also dehorned. But, according to animal protection laws, dehorning is permitted only if it is indispensable for the use to which the goat is put and if no veterinary considerations exist. Dehorning in adult animals should be done only by a veterinarian and under anesthesia. Kids can be dehorned by owners in the first week of life.

Consider carefully whether it is really necessary for you to keep unhorned goats and whether you

might not prefer to leave them their natural head ornaments.

Where to Buy Goats

For the beginner, it's a good idea to buy goats through the regional breeding association. The regional association will also put you in touch with the goat breeders in your area, from whom you can seek advice and discover where there are goat bucks for breeding.

Whether you buy your goat through a regional association or directly from a goat breeder without any intermediary, you should also

These three Boer kids are healthy and observant.

see the goat personally before your final decision to buy. An animal that is ailing and burdened with parasites can take away much of the pleasure of goat keeping.

How to Recognize a Healthy Goat

There are definite indications of sound health. A goat is healthy if it:
- eats well
- chews its cud
- is lively, alert, and sociable
- has a smooth, shining coat (in pastured goats and goats kept in a cold stall it is often somewhat shaggy)
- moves and jumps without hindrance
- is well nourished but not fat
- has clear, clean eyes
- has a cool, dry nose
- has mucous membranes well perfused with blood

- drops its feces in firm little balls
- has bright brown, clean urine.

The normal body temperature of a goat averages 102.2° to 104°F (39° to 40°C); the pulse averages 70 to 80 beats per minute (somewhat higher for kids).

Obviously, all these indications cannot be seen at first glance. Therefore, you should take a lot of time when you are buying and should observe the goat for a long period. You should also be aware of what may indicate indisposition or illness.

Consider carefully before buying a goat that:
- is thin
- arches its back
- favors a leg or limps
- has pale mucous membranes
- has a rough coat or bristly hairs, or is shedding
- has a swollen body
- has swollen limbs

This Boer kid is well nourished and stripped of its horns.

- has a discharge from its mouth, nose, or eyes
- has dried excrement actually on its tail or under it (indicates periodic diarrhea)
- has open sores or discharging lumps, especially below the ears and in front of the shoulders
- has long, pendulous udders and balloon teats.

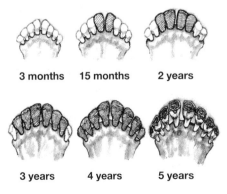

3 months	15 months	2 years

3 years	4 years	5 years

How to Determine Age

If the age of a goat is unknown, it may be determined by the appearance of the milk teeth as well as by the emergence of the second growth of teeth. At birth the innermost pair of incisors and often the second as well have already broken through. The remaining incisors follow at about the third month of life. At about 15 months the appearance of adult teeth begins; it is finished at three and a half to four years. At any given time, the adult goat possesses 12 molars in the upper and lower jaw and 8 incisors in the lower jaw only, whereas the upper

The age of a goat can be determined quite accurately by the development of the teeth as well as by how much they have been worn down.

These three Kiko kids have just been transported to the farm from market.

jaw is merely furnished with a horny plate. After the change of teeth is completed, the age of the goat can be estimated according to the progress of wear of the teeth.

Transporting Goats

When you have bought a goat, the next question is how to get it home. If you are on foot, most goats will allow themselves to be led easily on a rope attached to the collar—after a little initial resistance. Single goats, which are more often led this way, soon learn to enjoy such walking.

Goats may be transported over longer distances in any pickup or van, and if necessary, young goats and kids may even ride in the back-

seat of a passenger car. Standing, they balance there through all the turns of the vehicle.

Don't forget to tie the goats so that they can't leap about and jump into the lap of the driver! Unfortunately, they leave their mark everywhere in droppings and urine, so your human passengers will probably turn up their noses for weeks afterward. As a precaution, place the goat on a removable rubber mat that can be scrubbed with hot water and household cleaner.

A trailer is also useful for transporting goats, provided they are sheltered from the wind. Special adaptations for transporting small livestock are offered by various trailer manufacturers.

Chapter Four

Housing and Equipment

Stabling or Pasturing?

Pasturing exclusively is not possible year-round in the climate conditions prevailing in certain regions. Goats must be fed in the shed during five months or more of colder weather.

Let your goats spend at least several hours a day in the field from spring to fall. If you keep to the rules of field hygiene, the fresh air and sun will promote the good health of the goat.

Keeping goats entirely in the stable all year-round is possible, but then you should still allow your goats some regular exercise in the open, for which purpose a fenced yard is most suitable.

The Right Stable

The stable serves to protect the goats from the hardships of weather, from heat, cold, and rain. The form and the arrangement of the stable

A healthy buck rears up on its hind legs in order to see if he can climb over it.

should accommodate you but should also facilitate the movement of the goats, which will eat, drink, and be milked here. Furthermore, the births will often take place in the stable. If herds are not very large, a new building is usually not necessary for setting up a goat shed; an old building such as a former cow shed, a field shed, or a former garage can be used. Water and electrical connections are useful to have. The ceiling should be at least 8 feet (250 cm) high.

In a very high space, a loft can be added—for example, one made of logs—where straw bales can be stored. It is important to have enough draft-free air. Old cow sheds often still have a ventilating chimney and adjustable ventilators.

The Open Stable

A stable area in which the goat can move freely is best suited to the nature of the goat. Such an open stable is divided based on its two basic functions: a resting area, in which the goats can lie down to rest,

Three pregnant goats resting on a sawdust-covered observation stall.

and an eating area along the feeding shelf, where the goats can line up to eat.

If the goats go out to pasture regularly, at least in the summer season, you need 16 square feet (1.5 m²) free stable area per adult goat, of which almost 11 square feet (1 m²) is resting area. If the goats are to be kept in a shed all year long, you must figure on 21½ square feet (2 m²) to 27 square feet (2.5 m²) to give the goat enough room to move. Even better is an additional run outdoors. To avoid hygienic problems, this run must have a hard surface area that is easy to keep clean, such as cement blocks.

If you are keeping meat goats and the kids are allowed to stay with the mother for very long, you must provide for their additional space requirements when you plan the goat shed. Figure about 5½ square feet (0.5 m²) per kid.

Allow a space 15½ inches (40 cm) wide for eating at the feeding shelf, which should be reachable from outside so that the goats needn't go through the stable section to feed. Raised resting places are especially beloved by goats. Therefore, you should at least put a large upside-down box in their resting area, or, if space permits, attach to the wall a run-around wooden resting bench 23 to 31 inches (60 to 80 cm) wide at a height of about 31 inches (80 cm).

Partitions

A paling fence of vertically placed laths or boards, which should be 2 inches (5 cm) from the floor at most, is best for defining and separating

Goats are perfectly able to get along with other farm animals, such as chickens and cats.

the shed sections. The space between the laths must not be larger than 2 inches (5 cm) so that the goats can't put their heads through and the kids can't slip through. The partition must be at least 47 inches (120 cm) high so that no goat can possibly get over it. Add some horizontal laths to the upper edge to keep the goats from getting their necks caught between the vertical laths and strangling if they stand up

This photograph shows a typical example of a feeding shelf and shelter.

against the fence and stick their heads over.

Horizontally placed cross laths and posts must be stable enough to withstand the weight of goats butting against them.

Such a wooden fence is of course not as permanent as a galvanized metal construction, but it is far cheaper and always easy to repair.

Floor and Litter

The floor is best made of cement, but it can also be made of brick paving or wooden planks.

The place in the feeding area where the goats stand along the feeding shelf should be only lightly littered and swept out daily.

Separate the hay-littered resting area from the feeding area with a sill—for example, a wooden beam—or by raising the eating area.

Straw is the best litter, but you can also use sawdust or peat. With regular littering, a straw-manure mattress develops under the goats' feet. It sucks up the urine completely and needs to be removed only rarely. About 1 pound (0.5 kg) of straw per goat per day is needed. If you want to buy the littering straw only once yearly, you will need storage space for baled straw of almost 4 cubic yards (3 m^3) per goat.

Since a well-tended straw-manure mattress needs to be turned out every three months, it's best if you can organize it so that the manure can be taken directly to the garden or the fields. Additional fertilizer is then not necessary.

If immediate removal is not possible, you need approximately 11 square feet (1 m^2) per goat for a manure storage area and possibly also 0.6 cubic yards (0.45 m^3) of space for a dung-water trench.

The Feeding Shelf

In many traditional stables the hay and green feed are placed in a rack. With their picky way of eating, the goats pull out a lot of feed, which then falls on the ground and is spoiled. They also stand with their forefeet in the racks or even jump right into racks that are fastened low down. In this way they foul the feed with the dung stuck to their hoofs and thus promote the transmission of internal parasites. Narrow troughs are also not very suitable. In these the fodder sticks together, much to the goats' dislike. They then just shove the whole wad of fodder out of the troughs with their heads.

A *feeding shelf* is therefore best for offering food. It is attached outside the stall area in front of the feeding gate. The goat stretches its head through this gate and can sort and sift through the feed on the broad shelf but cannot damage it.

You can easily make the feeding shelf yourself out of wood; it is far less expensive than a cement feeding trough. A width of 19½ inches (50 cm) has been shown to be good; still, if there is space enough, the surface may even be a little wider. Finish the edges with boards so that the goats can't easily push off or pull down the feed. Screw the shelf firmly to the feeding gate and prop it

Minerals are important to the health of goats.

up further by adding legs under the surface or simply placing a few cement blocks underneath.

The shelf should also not be attached too low, or the goats will place their front feet in it and can foul the fodder. If you want to be able to shift it higher, provide a few more screw holes for attaching it to the feeding gate. Then you can adjust the height of the shelf as the goats grow and are able to stand higher.

If a change of the standing level is not anticipated, a firmly attached feed shelf at a height of 15½ to 19½ inches (40 to 50 cm) is appropriate for large goats. Even smaller goats and young ones can manage this level without difficulty if at the 10-inch (15-cm) level you add a step ¾ to 1 inch (2 to 3 cm) wide on which they can support themselves with their front feet.

The Feeding Gate

The feeding gate separates the feeding shelf from the standing area. It should keep the goat from climbing up and over the feeding table or from pulling out extra feed that is then spoiled. By separating individual

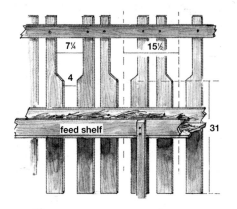

feed shelf

7¼ 15½ 4 31

feeding places, it also keeps each goat from disturbing the ones on either side while eating. Frequently, the feeding gate also functions to hold the goat in place if you want to milk her or carry out a treatment.

There are many forms of feeding gate, and some of them are wasteful and expensive. Because the eating slots in the lower section are small, the goats must lift their heads in order to free themselves. Thus, the goats are generally kept from pulling down the feed and letting it fall on the floor. With the help of a simple drop bar, you can hold the goat in the feeding gate. The drop bar should be fastened up and down as well with a bolt or peg, because goats soon figure out how they can lift it and slip out.

Racks

In addition to the feeding shelf, you can also attach a rack in the resting area, which you fill with straw or inferior hay. The goats search in it for what tastes good to them, and the rest falls right onto the floor as litter. This rack should hang as high as possible so that the goats can't reach it with their front feet. Goats are very agile, and the upright posture fits their natural way of eating from bushes and trees. Racks can be made of wood or metal. The distance between the struts should be about 2 inches (5 cm).

Also provide a strong hook at a height of at least 79 inches (2 m) on which you can hang a bundle of leafy branches, the favorite food of goats.

Licks

Fasten mineral licks in the same way at least 59 inches (1.5 m) high on the wall, so that the goats will not step on them with their front feet as they walk.

Watering

Fresh, clean drinking water must always be available for free access. In smaller herds the water can be made available in a pail. Two to 10½ quarts (2 to 10 L) per goat per day are necessary, depending on milk yield and the water content of the feed. Because a container standing on the floor is easily tipped over, however, and becomes fouled by dung and urine, it must be changed at least twice daily.

Far more hygienic are self-operated troughs, of which there is one especially designed for goats. Those used for cattle are not suitable. The self-operated trough must be placed high enough to avoid being fouled by dung and urine. But even so, it must be checked daily for cleanliness and functioning. One self-service drinking trough will take care of up to 20 animals. For stables in which temperatures fall below freezing, there are electrically heated water troughs.

Windows and Doors

The window surface should amount to ⅕ to ½₀ of the stable area. Simple tilting windows are completely satisfactory. During the summer months they will be taken off the hinges entirely.

The doors of the shed sections are made to open inward, toward the goats. This makes it more difficult for the animals to leave their section whenever the door is open. The door is best fastened with a strong and not easily turned bolt, since goats show an altogether astonishing facility for opening closed doors.

The Right Stable Climate

The stabled goat's climate requirements are not great. Goats prefer a temperature between 46° and 59°F (8° and 15°C). If they are protected from drafts and their resting place is

A goat drinking from its water bowl. Clean water should be available at all times.

warm and dry, they will even bear the cold at below-freezing temperatures well. Very young kids are the exception. The goat is extremely sensitive to dampness. A humidity between 60 and 85 percent is optimal.

If in winter, because of your human need for warmth, you make all the cracks as airtight as possible, the humidity rises, but also the level of harmful gases in the stable air, especially of ammonia, rises. The goats can get respiratory ailments, which then may wrongly be termed "colds" caused by the decreased warmth. If the walls and the water pipes in the stable begin to sweat and make the sharp smell of dung and urine more noticeable, you should ventilate more often, even if

the temperature in the shed falls a little as a result. Goats adapt to raw climate conditions as they occur and will grow a winter coat as a rule. If in winter you take goats out of a warm shed into the cold, you must accomplish the change step by step, so that the animals have the opportunity to get used to the difference in temperature.

The Mother–Child Area

If the kids of milk goats are to be left with their mothers for some days, you need a mother–child section for them. But meat-goat mothers, especially those having young for the first time, also get on better if they are alone with their kids in the first few days after birth. Therefore, a section of the shed should be partitioned off with a paling fence. Naturally, the

mothers must be fed there regularly and be able to drink water, so it is handier if you plan ahead of time for a special area for mothers and young in which there are both an eating place for the mothers and a drinking trough. An area of about 21½ square feet (2 m²) is enough; it should be completely strewn with litter.

The Feeding Shelf

If the kids are to remain in this section for longer than a week after birth, they must also have access to feed and water. Therefore, the feeding shelf can only be at a height of about 8 inches (20 cm). Attach a horizontal board with butterfly screws so that the small kids can't slip through the feeding gate. The mother goat bends over the board to the feeding table; the little ones put their heads underneath.

At the beginning, a clearance of 6 inches (15 cm) under the board is enough. A row of screw holes makes it possible to move the board up as the kid grows. After three to four weeks, when the kids are too large to be able to slip through the eating slot, the horizontal board can be removed. This way the kid will also share in the food without the mother's eating the kid's share.

The Watering Trough

The drinking water must be set up so that the kids can reach it. But this also means that it will be easily fouled and so must be even more carefully checked than the higher-placed watering troughs in the adult goat areas.

The Nurturing Area

If the kids are going to be raised in their own section, they should also eat there through an eating gate. As already mentioned, a feeding trough inside the area is too easily fouled with dung and urine.

You should estimate a space of 5½ square feet (0.5 m²) per kid and a feeding shelf length of 8 inches (20 cm).

After they stop nursing, the kids can be moved for further nurturing to a young goat section that in dimensions and execution largely conforms to the open stable of the adult goats. For each young goat, figure on 10¾ square feet (1 m²) of area and 12 inches (30 cm) of feeding shelf length.

How many different shed areas you need depends on the number of mother goats, how quickly the births follow each other, and how long you are keeping the kids. For hygienic reasons, you should be able to install kids only a few weeks old or newborn in their own freshly cleaned section, and must not add older kids. On the other hand, the raising of groups of kids of about the same age is generally without problems.

The Buck Stable

If you are keeping a buck for breeding, the stable must be adjusted to his strength, which he uses, especially during the mating season. For bucks the open stable is also preferable to the tethered one. The walls of the buck area must be particularly rugged. In addition to being sturdily constructed, the wall must be high enough to discourage the buck's attempts to escape. To be safe, the walls should be a minimum of 5 feet (150 cm) high.

Most bucks get along well with several others in one section. You must figure 33 square feet (3 m²) of resting area per buck and about 54 square feet (5 m²) of run, preferably out of doors.

The Tethered Stable

If your space is very limited, you will have to decide on a tethered stable. Here the goat is tied to the eating place and has a space requirement of 24 by 47 inches (60 by 120 cm).

The eating area in the tethered shed is also the resting place and must be cleaned out daily; the straw requirements for this are somewhat less than in the open stable. The floor of packed chalk 6 inches (15 cm) thick in the eating-resting area is best finished with an insulating covering such as straw or wood shavings. The standing area should have a slight incline toward the rear and be bounded by a gutter leading to a collecting ditch.

Woven wire goat fences are necessary to keep your goats from wandering off on their own.

The feeding shelf is arranged the same way as in the open stable. A feeding gate is not necessary for a tethered goat but is recommended so that goats on either side disturb each other less while they are eating.

The tethered stable is encountered in many traditional small farms, but it is not suited to the nature of the goat. Choose it only if your space situation truly allows no other solution. Most of the existing tethered stables can be converted to open stables at very little expense.

The Pasture and Its Equipment

Fencing

If the goats are not going to be tended in the pasture, they must be kept by suitable arrangements from running away, trampling fresh pasturage, or injuring vegetable gardens or fruit trees. *A fence of vertical wooden palings* 47 inches (120 cm) high, with a maximum distance between the slats of 2 inches (5 cm) and a maximum distance from the ground of 2 inches (5 cm), is largely goat-proof. This cannot be said of many other fences. Wire mesh fences and knotted wire fences, which are useful for sheep paddocks, will over time be trampled down by goats with their front feet. Horned goats love to play tug-of-war on the wire of these fences with their horns.

Barbed wire fences become very expensive since many barbs must be placed at narrow intervals. Besides, the danger of injury is great because the goats try again and again, in spite of everything, to get over the wire.

Electric fencing has been used with varying success. Many goat

keepers have had satisfactory experience with electric fences such as those used for sheep. Electric tapes work better than wires. Nevertheless, there are always some goats that will get over even an electric fence. Therefore, limit the installation of electric fence as much as possible to the changeable subdivision of the pasture and also erect a strong fence as an outside limit; this must be inspected regularly and repaired as necessary.

The wooden fence is ideal as an outer boundary, but often it is out of the question because of cost. Usually the cheaper knotted wire fence is used, which of course is in need of repair more often.

Tethering

If you have only a few goats and a not very large pasture area, tethering makes more sense than installing an expensive fence. For this you use as a ground anchor a strong iron post, at least 23 inches (60 cm) long, of builder's steel, for example. A light steel chain about 79 inches (2 m) long is fastened to this anchor with a ring, and the other end is attached to the goat's collar with a closed hook. There must be a swivel between chain and ring and also on the collar hook to prevent the chain from getting wound around.

Another way of tethering is to run a wire between two pegs at least 79 inches (2 m) apart from each other;

the chain ring of one or several goats runs along this wire.

Shelter

If goats are going to be outside in the pasture all day without supervision, they need a light shelter that will protect them from wind and rain and also from strong sunlight. Such a structure need only be closed on the weather side, and you can make it yourself inexpensively out of wooden planks.

Protection for Fruit Trees

When there are fruit trees in the area, you must protect them from being gnawed on by the goats. Peeling of the bark from the trunks is especially damaging. You can best prevent this by building an enclosure of wooden laths around the tree.

Chapter Five

Feeding

The goat needs nutrients for its maintenance and mobility, for growth and milk production. Like sheep and cattle, it is a ruminant. Its special digestive apparatus allows it to use foodstuffs such as grass and leaves that cannot be used by non-ruminant animals and humans. The large rumen of the goat is especially important in this process. It works like a fermentation chamber in which the bacteria are broken down along with the constituents of the food. The healthy coexistence of these microorganisms with the host goat is a well-balanced equilibrium and must always be taken into consideration when feeding.

Fundamentals of Goat Nutrition

Anyone who has grown up working with goats can intuitively satisfy their manifold feeding requirements without knowing in detail about the biological particulars of ruminant nourishment.

As a beginner, you unfortunately cannot rely on such a treasury of experience and must take the trouble to gain an understanding of the digestive requirements of cud-chewing goats. The nutrients must be considered in relation to the particular needs of the ruminant, as well as the feeding and grazing behavior of the goat in particular. First you must understand the biological fundamentals, which then serve as the basis for proper feeding.

The Digestion

A ruminant (or cud-chewing animal) like the sheep and the cow, the goat can take in a large quantity of food in a very short time, which it swallows with very little chewing; then, during a subsequent resting period, the goat carefully reduces the food to smaller pieces with a second chewing. For animals in the wild this is a protection since it can diminish the grazing time, during which they are exposed to predators and are less alert because they are eating. Then for chewing their cud they withdraw to a safe place—a hiding place or, which goats prefer,

A Nubian kid grazing in a field.

a high, hard-to-reach place with a good view of the surroundings.

The Rumen

Ruminants have a four-chambered stomach that makes chewing cud possible; the first three chambers are the rumen, the reticulum, and the omasum. The true stomach, in which the hydrochloric acid and digestive enzymes are secreted, is the abomasum or rennet stomach, which adjoins the omasum. In the rumen the food is mechanically broken down, mixed, and fermented. The rumen is still undeveloped in the newborn kid and much more of the milk passes through a stomach canal directly into the rennet stomach, where it is digested by the action of the enzyme rennin. Therefore, the kid is basically not a ruminant in the first weeks of its life; only

with the intake of roughage does the rumen begin to enlarge.

The rumen is the largest compartment of the stomachs. In an adult goat it has a volume of about 10½ quarts (10 L). You can tell when it is filled with feed by the disappearance of the "hunger cavity" in front of the left hip bone.

Breakdown of Cellulose

In the rumen are bacteria and other microorganisms. Only these are able to break down cellulose. This is the energy-rich fiber substance of food plants that the goat cannot use for nourishment without the help of these microorganisms. The products of the cellulose breakdown are fatty acids, which are absorbed into the blood through the walls of the rumen for further utilization by the goat. In addition, this

digestion produces carbon dioxide and methane gas, which are expelled through the mouth in a belch.

Albumin Production

The protein albumin in the food is also broken down in the rumen. This process produces ammonia, which the bacteria then reuse for synthesis of their own protein. This bacterial protein is very high grade; it will be utilized by the goat when the bacteria pass from the rumen into the intestine and are digested there.

Occasional excesses of ammonia enter the bloodstream but return in a circuit through the liver and saliva back to the rumen. By means of this recycling, the goat makes full use of the albumin in the fodder. It can synthesize albumin of the highest biological value in milk and in meat,

even from feed of poorer quality. With the help of the bacteria, the goat is able to synthesize albumin from other nitrogen-containing food substances as well, for example, urea. The microorganisms also create B vitamins and vitamin K in the rumen, so that the goat is not dependent on the supply of these vitamins in the feed.

Rumen Function

When chewing its cud, the goat regurgitates a mouthful of the contents of the rumen. It carefully breaks this down by chewing and mixes it with saliva to facilitate the work of the microorganisms.

The muscular walls of the rumen contract regularly so that the rumen contents are well mixed and sufficient quantities of digested nutrients are expelled into the omasum and further into the abomasum and the intestine. Without this movement the digestion of the rumen would come to a standstill, a life-threatening situation for the goat. These movements are induced by roughage, which stimulates the walls of the rumen.

The rumen can perform its unique fermentation function only when
• the feed is coarse enough
• the feed contains a minimum of starch and sugar
• rumen acidity fluctuates as little as possible.

The easily soluble carbohydrates provide the microorganisms with energy and stimulate them to work to break down the cellulose as well as to synthesize high-quality protein and vitamin B. The daily quantity of this energy provider can be small, but the supply of it must be regular. Thus, the composition of the feed ration is determined not only by nutrient requirements but also by its effect on the function of the rumen.

The food will be further broken down in the rennin stomach and in the small intestine. The body of the goat absorbs the nutrients resulting from digestion partly in the rumen but mainly in the small intestine. The indigestible elements of feed are concentrated in the large intestine and then excreted.

The Nutrients

The following nutrients must be contained in the fodder of the goat:
- energy-yielding nutrients
- albumin
- minerals and vitamins.

In addition, roughage is very important.

Energy-yielding Nutrients

The energy contained in the feed will be only partly utilized by the goat. One portion leaves the body again in the form of undigested nutrients in the dung, another portion as urea in the urine, and another as methane from the rumen. The energy the goat actually uses goes partly to maintain correct body function and to move. Only what remains is utilized for growth and for production of milk.

The goat gets its energy primarily from starch, sugar, and cellulose. The energy contained in starch and sugar is easily and quickly available, whereas the cellulose must first be broken down by the microorganisms of the rumen.

The energy produced from the breakdown of protein is comparatively little. Fat usually plays no role in the feed of the goat.

Albumin

Also, only part of the albumin in feed is utilized; the rest is excreted in dung and urine. By recycling the ammonia from the albumin breakdown in the rumen, the goat can make use of a scant supply of protein very economically.

Minerals and Vitamins

Domestic goats, because of their quick growth and their high milk production, have a high mineral requirement, which is not entirely filled by the basic feed. This is true in nature, for wild goats also love a salt lick and sometimes eat mineral-rich soil. The most important minerals are calcium and phosphorus. Trace elements, such as sodium and magnesium, are also necessary in smaller quantities.

Vitamin deficiency seldom occurs in adult goats, because the B vitamins are synthesized by the microorganisms of the rumen and vitamin C is manufactured by the goat itself. In young kids, in which the rumen is not yet working, adding B vitamins directly to the diet in the form of yeast is recommended.

Roughage

The term *roughage* denotes the cell-wall components of food plants, of which cellulose constitutes the largest part. Fine young leaves contain little coarse fiber. But the older the plant and the larger and stronger the stalks and leaves, the greater the fiber content.

A high content of coarse fiber means that the nutrients in this feed will not be immediately available to the goat. First, the cellulose of the plant cell walls must be broken down by the microorganisms in the rumen of the goat. Only then can the goat use the resulting fatty acids for energy production. Furthermore, the nutrients contained within the plant cells themselves can only be completely available to the goat if the cell walls are broken down.

Since the fat in goat's milk is synthesized from the fatty acids produced by the breakdown of cellulose in the rumen, an increase of roughage in the diet increases the fat content of the milk.

The more rough fiber that food plants contain, the coarser they are. The goats must chew such feed longer, which stimulates the flow of saliva. The saliva neutralizes the acids in the rumen and thereby creates conditions that particularly favor the rumen's microorganisms. In addition, the coarse plant parts stimulate the rumen walls to regular contractions.

It is clear from all this that roughage in the diet is very important for healthy digestion. However, in old feed plants the roughage content is so high that their digestion in the rumen may take an undesirably long time. Also, if the plants are at all woody, the nutrients may be only partly broken down by the rumen microorganisms.

Types of Feed

Pasturage

Goats prefer to feed in pastures in which there are many different grasses and weeds growing. With somewhat more difficulty they may get used to fields that are all grass, and only then if they find enough of the tasty types of meadow grass. Ornamental lawns are not suitable for goat pastures. On the other hand, field banks and roadsides, with their variety of plants, are usually very agreeable to goats. Bushy meadows are not commonly found in most cultivated American and European countrysides, unfortunately. Fallow land and areas that have been allowed to go wild are excellent goat pastures. Of course, they then look even wilder than before. Orchards should be used as goat pasture only if you protect the bark of younger trees from being stripped and if you accept that the foliage will be eaten

Goat owners can help with the feeding of their goats by cutting up green plant matter and setting it out.

up to a height of about 70 inches (180 cm). Be careful about using chemical pesticides on the fruit trees! After a chemical treatment, wait the length of time recommended on the package, at the very minimum, before you allow the goats to graze under the trees. It is strongly recommended, however, that you give very serious consideration to the complete avoidance of chemical pesticides, at least during the grazing season.

Grain fields may also be used for goat pastures, as long as the seed heads are not yet showing. Grazing induces the young wheat plants to produce more leaves. This will compensate for any possible injury from chewing.

Farmers who want to avoid using chemical weed killers can make use of the goat's preference for weedy plants. Goats will purposefully graze out weeds like thistles, for example. On the other hand, they have less use for grasses, which include the grains.

Green Fodder in the Stable

Feed that has been cut from the meadow is usually used for feeding in the stable. But green fodder can also be grown in fields and in the garden. The weeds that grow there can also be used for fodder. Green leaves and evergreen branches can also be fed in the stable.

Meadow Fodder

Feed that cannot be grazed directly is cut and offered to the goat in the stable. Usually the feed gets a little dirty in the mowing, and therefore the food value of a given quantity of fodder is diminished.

Cultivated Fodder

Food that is grown in fields and gardens can also be used along with the meadow fodder; this consists primarily of clover varieties but also green corn and sunflower leaves. It pays to grow such green crops in every vegetable garden in alternation with the vegetable culture. This way you always have some feed quickly at hand, and at the same time this practice will promote productive soil and plant health. The recommended agricultural practice of alternating crops of grain with food plants from the family of the Cruciferae, such as rape, mustard, and cabbages, is less suited to crop rotation in the vegetable garden. A portion of the leaves of corn plants and beets can be plucked before the harvest without diminishing the size of the kernels or the beet too much. If you are going to feed the corn stems, you must cut them in little pieces, about 0.8 inches (2 cm) long.

What Not to Feed

Do not feed yew branches, since in even the smallest quantities this evergreen is lethal to goats! Leaves of stone fruit trees, like plums, cherries, peaches, and such, may be used only very fresh or very dry, but never wilted, or prussic acid (cyanide) poisoning can occur. Sorghums and Sudan grass are also cyanogenic, as are common milkweed, horse nettle, black nightshade, mountain laurel, milo, and hemp, among others.

Weeds

Everything that is a weedy nuisance in the garden can be offered to goats, which will pick out the tastiest plant parts. They especially love thistles, bindweed, and goatsfoot. These particularly stubborn weeds are much less trying if you can use them as fodder.

Leafy and Needled Branches

Green, leafy branches can be cut from all our native trees and hung in the stable. You will soon find out whether your goats have a preference for a particular kind of tree. In smaller quantities, you can also offer evergreen branches, which are healthy for goats, especially in winter when there is no other green feed available.

Winter Feed

Feed reserves must be laid in against the time when no green feed is available. Green feed can be dried as hay or fermented as silage.

To justify the labor-intensive production of these fodder reserves and the expensive storage space, especially for silage, you must see to it that you have the highest possible quality of feed. You will achieve this by early cutting. Feed to be used for silage should be cut about the middle of May; feed to be made into hay, at the end of May to the beginning of June—at the latest, when the grasses are beginning to bloom. Then the feed has the best nutrient content.

The second mowing is less dependent on proper timing, since it

A kid unable to stand as a result of a mineral deficiency.

is more luxuriant and is very quickly gathered. Furthermore, you will achieve a good quality of feed if you avoid destroying the nutrients in the preparation of hay and silage.

Hay

The ground drying of hay takes three to four days of dry, warm weather. The grass is mowed close with a machine or a scythe. Since hay preparation usually occurs under pressure of time because of the weather, it pays, even for small areas, to procure a tractor-driven mowing bar. The rows of mown feed are gathered up either mechanically or by hand with a fork and evenly divided. During the first few days the feed is turned as often as possible, twice at the very least. By hand, this is best done with a rake. By evening, the already-dried fodder sticks up in small, thin rows. When the dew dries

the next morning, these rows will again be divided.

The further the drying proceeds, the more carefully the hay must be turned to avoid crumbling the nutrient-rich leaves. In very good weather the hay is dried to some 20 percent of its water content by the afternoon of the second day and can be brought in. You can tell if it's dry enough when the tufts are no longer easy to draw into a rope but tear apart with very little effort. If the hay is not yet dry enough by the evening of the second day, put it into thick rows or pile it in heaps, which the next day will be spread out again. Depending on the weather, a fourth drying day may even be necessary.

If rain threatens, pile the hay in heaps; otherwise the nutrients leach out too quickly in its wilted condition.

Hay storage space: To lessen the weather risks, on larger goat holdings it pays to erect an airy storage place for hay. Here the hay can be stored when the water content is down to only 40 percent. You can tell the water content has sunk to 40 percent when the hay begins to rustle. A further important advantage of this method is that the hay undergoes less mechanical handling and therefore suffers less damage from crumbling.

Drying frames: Even on a small goat farm the weather risks and crumbling damage can be diminished if you dry the hay in a frame after it has been wilted on the ground. This type of haymaking was widely practiced in earlier times, and today, too, if you are working by hand with a fork and rake, it saves work to pack the already-dried hay onto the drying rack on the second day or even on the first. A good rack is the hay hut, which you can construct easily and cheaply with wooden posts. Other forms of drying racks are the three-legged rack, the Swedish rack (a drying fence of stretched wire), and the post rack. Swedish racks and post racks can even be loaded with freshly mown feed, if it is packed loosely enough. The hay dries on the rack without further work and without crumbling damage and, depending on the weather, can be stored in the course of two to four weeks. If the top layer is packed neatly and thickly as a cap, even steady rain will not penetrate it.

Since the stored hay still must go through a sweating process, it may be fed six to eight weeks after harvest, at the earliest. Hay that has been mechanically pressed into bales requires less storage space.

Leafy branches: You can hang these branches, loosely bundled, under the roof to dry to use later for leaf fodder.

Silage

For fermentation in a silo, green feed, sometimes wilted for half a day, must be cut very fine and be compressed. The machines and buildings necessary for this do not pay for the small goat keeper, so the siloing of green feed is completely

Kashmiri-type buck (left) and Sannen doe (right).

out of the question. On the other hand, leftover fruit can be turned into excellent silage. Mash the fruit in some kind of acid-fast container—for example, a plastic barrel—that you can make as nearly airtight as possible. After six to eight weeks you have ready for use an aromatic feed that goats love.

Roots and Tubers

Other important winter feeds are potatoes, turnips, and rape, which you can store either in a dry cellar or in a pit in the ground until spring.

Straw

Also used for winter feed is the straw from grain and legumes, which is ready for storage when it is dropped during the harvest of the kernels.

Concentrated Feed

Feedstuffs are described as concentrated feed when, because of their small water content, they offer easily digested nutrients in concentrated form, especially grain and grain products, legumes, and the residues of vegetable oil production.
• Wheat kernels, usually fed shredded or crushed, are particularly important, because with their starch content they are the best providers of easily accessible energy.
• Residues of vegetable oil production, such as soybean mash, linseed meal, or coconut cake, are especially rich in protein.
• Legumes such as peas and field beans contain starch as an energy source but at the same time have a moderate protein content.
• Grain products left over after milling, such as wheat bran, are less easily digested because of the high roughage content but to make up for it are rich in protein and vitamin B.
• Molasses and molasses cake are the residue of the beet-sugar production process. They offer easily accessible energy very inexpensively.

You can buy concentrated feed either as a single feed item or as a mixture, which is usually pelleted, that is, has been pressed into small, round little pieces. The goats prefer this form to the meal form.

Kitchen Scraps

In principle, you can feed kitchen scraps to your goat. You must, however, be extremely careful that the scraps are not dirty, fermented, or moldy.

Feed Supplements

Usually the necessary vitamins, minerals, and medications are not administered separately but are bought as a so-called premixture or are already mixed into concentrated feed. Mineral mixtures are available as meal for mixing into concentrated feed or in solid form in licking dishes or as licking stones.

When using mineral feed for goats, you must be careful that it has adequate copper. You can use the feed used for cattle. Special mineral feed for goats is now available everywhere, but mineral feed for sheep also conforms to the requirements for goats, except that it has less copper. Too low of a copper content places goats at risk for deficiency.

The mixing of dried medicinal and seasoning herbs in the concentrated food promotes the appetite and the health of goats. Such mixtures are available in the feed stores.

Grazing and Feeding Behavior

How the Goat Feeds

The ruminants can be divided into two large groups according to their eating habits: the coarse-feed eaters and the tender-feed-selecting animals.

Coarse-feed eaters such as cattle and sheep eat grass and weeds from the ground, proceeding not very selectively and ingesting the largest possible amount.

The tender-feed-selecting animals include many gazelle and antelope species. They take up smaller quantities of food, but they therefore seek out the most nourishing parts of the plant, such as young shoots, small leaves, and blossoms in grass, weeds, bushes, and trees.

The goat is classified between these two groups. What is remarkable is that obviously goats can adapt to the available food supply with one or the other feeding pattern. You should not require too much of this adaptability, however,

especially because the rumen changes over slowly.

The particular grazing and feeding behavior of the goat can be better understood if we consider the original habitat of the goat, the mountains. Here, in the region of the tree line, there is a great abundance of vegetation, from the grasses and weeds of the alpine meadow, to the bushes of the transition zone, to the deciduous and evergreen trees of the forest. During the summer there is enough to eat, but in winter there is little available: dried grass and leaves, withered branches, bark, and evergreen plant parts (for example, the needles of conifers).

The wild goat adapted itself wonderfully to these two very different feeding situations. In summer it utilized the multiple offerings as well as possible, in that it harvested the food richest in nutrients. With the poor food supply of the winter, it had to try out the edibility of whatever it could find and be content with food poor in nutrients.

This explains the contradiction between the goat's reputation as an extraordinarily picky and nibbling eater and its being often praised for being easily satisfied.

The Picky Goat

If you observe a goat that is eating, it is not always easy to explain why it chooses just this or that plant. Nevertheless, it is generally true that the goat prefers the leaves of bushes, trees, and weed plants to

Dogs like this Border Collie make excellent guards for goats.

grass. The goat likes to eat a mixture of all these plant types and does not fundamentally reject grass.

Of course you can accustom your goat to an all-grass pasture, but you need good nerves for it. Despite its hunger, it will stand bleating in the field for the whole day if the feed does not meet with its approval. When the goat finally does acquiesce to the inevitable, the quantity of food it takes will still be less than usual.

Something similar holds true for the waste of feed. Figure that the goat will leave about 30 percent of a satisfactory offering of average green feed or hay. If you don't want to put up with this waste, you can pressure the goat into being less fussy by diminishing the size of the portion. But this will make the animal eat less

overall. You need to find a middle way between these extremes. In any case, it pays to meet the goat halfway and to offer it as varied a feed ration as possible.

The Nibbling Goat

A goat can also inflict damage with its nibbling habits. If it gets into the vegetable garden, it will not just eat a head or two of lettuce until it is full but may perhaps just nibble out the heart of each head of lettuce or bite off the growing spike of each cabbage plant. Such behavior has given the goat a reputation for limitless appetite, perhaps incorrectly.

The Easily Satisfied Goat

The ease of satisfying the goat's needs should not be overestimated.

Goats have a high nutrient need, the mother animal for the production of milk and the young animals for growth. For this reason, even in the wild, goats developed a form of adaptation to the scarcity of food in winter by confining births to spring.

The fact that goats often are in markedly better body condition in poor pastures than the sheep and cows that graze there at the same time, or that there are only goats there at all, does not mean that goats do not have needs. Goats fare better than other ruminants because they know much better how to choose the most nutritional feed out of a poorer offering. This is especially true of pastures with a large portion of brush.

The often-heard observation that goats can utilize coarse fiber feed better than sheep and cattle can, and that on the same quantity of feed they produce more milk than cows do, must unfortunately be banished to the realm of fable.

Behavior in the Pasture

If a goat arrives at the pasture hungry, it begins to eat without stopping. After its first hunger is assuaged, its manner of eating becomes increasingly less steady. It nibbles here a little, there a little, and increasingly searches out only the especially tasty weeds and leaves. It can be easily distracted from eating, whether by a bird flying past or by a leaf that moves in the wind.

Goats do not like rain in the pasture. At the very first drop they stop eating and shake their heads. If they are not able to leave the meadow and find shelter, they complain with loud bleating. Only when it rains for a long period of time and the goat has become extremely hungry will it resume its grazing even in the rain.

To eat from bushes and trees, the goat stands on its hind legs, props itself with its front legs or stands free, and tries to reach the leaves with neck outstretched. With its long and flexible tongue, it snatches at leaves that it can't quite reach with its mouth.

The goat even eats the leaves of plants that have stickers or thorns, such as those of the wild rose or the blackthorn. In this it seems to use its flexible upper lip, for the most part, but eats so fast that exact observation is difficult.

Feeding

Basics

"The eye of the master fattens his cattle." This biblical wisdom applies especially to the goat. Consider the following questions:
• How long and how often does the goat eat?
• Is its rumen well filled?
• Does it chew its cud?
• What feed does it like best? What feed does it avoid?

- Does the goat gain weight or lose weight?
- How does its coat look?
- Is the goat lively?
- Is the dung formed into almost-round balls?
- Has the milk production changed?

Your observations, along with basic knowledge of the details of food intake and the digestion of the goat as well as of the nutrient content in the feed, will help you to adjust the feed accordingly. Even if the composition of the feed does not exactly meet the requirements of the goat, the animal is usually able to manage with it.

For goats with a higher milk production, of course, only a small deviation from the optimal nutrient content of the feed ration is permissible, since otherwise you risk a decrease in the milk production or even injury to the goat's health. Thus, even if you must be careful about the economics of your goat keeping, you must still calculate the feed portions precisely. You can also have an agricultural station examine the feed for nutrient content.

When feeding, you should keep three basic principles in mind at all times:

1. Use basic feed of high quality

2. Keep the composition varied

3. Allow a sufficiently long time to feed.

This way you will obtain the highest possible intake of food.

The Principal Importance of the Energy Supply

A goat with a good milk production has a high nutrient requirement for some three months after the birth of kids. Only with effort can she ingest with the feed as many nutrients as she needs for milk production and her own nourishment. If she doesn't meet this requirement, a nutrient deficiency develops. This primarily affects the goat's supply of energy, with the albumin supply affected to a lesser extent, since the goat utilizes the protein in fodder particularly economically during malnourishment.

The goat tries to compensate for a nutrient deficiency with the breakdown of body reserves, which, since she is only marginally in the position to build up body reserves, she can accomplish only in very small measure. Furthermore, during the rapid breakdown of body fat, an excess of so-called ketone bodies can develop, a condition that brings on the life-threatening disorder known as ketosis.

Therefore, during the time of high milk production, a high nutrient intake is especially important, with strict attention paid to providing for the supply of enough energy.

The Right Feed for Ruminants

To be right for ruminants, the feed must contain enough roughage. Coarse fiber such as grass, weeds, and hay provides this requirement, as long as it is not a very young growth.

During high milk production, roughage alone cannot supply the goat with enough nutrients, because the rumen's capacity for the intake of this voluminous feed is limited. Then you must feed with additional nutrient-rich concentrated feed. Concentrated feed is low in coarse fiber and contains energy primarily in the form of starch. To correctly feed it to ruminants despite this lack of roughage, you must give the concentrated feed in the smallest possible portions. Any kind of feed change—whether you increase the concentrated feed ration, for example, or change the feed from grass to clover—should be accomplished slowly and by degrees, in order to give the microorganisms in the rumen time to adjust.

Seasonal Changes in Feeding

Spring and Summer

The basic feed is the young growth of the fodder, whether it is fed in the pasture or in the stable. This feed is readily digested and has a high protein content. All the same, it should not be used alone; otherwise, an excess of protein will develop, along with a deficiency of energy and roughage. This imbalance aggravates an already-existing condition in most milk goats just at this time of year, an energy deficit because of their high

Leafy branches are part of the proper diet for goats. In summer, the branches should be fresh; in winter, they should be dried. You can hang them in the stable or spread them out in a pasture.

Typical Daily Feed Ration of a Milk Goat in Spring and Summer

Pasture/field fodder	13.2 lb (6.0 kg)
Meadow hay	1.1 lb (0.5 kg)
Molasses chips	2.2 lb (1.0 kg)
Barley straw	as wanted
Fresh branches	small supplements

milk production and the fact that concentrated and roughage-rich supplementary feedstuffs are only limitedly at their disposal.

Turnips and potatoes are good feed, insofar as they are available in spring. Best are molasses chips, of which a goat can eat as much as 2.2 pounds (1 kg) daily. In addition, you should offer good hay or even straw to make up the roughage portion. This way the goats will manage with the young fodder growth without health problems and can utilize the good protein supply most efficiently.

I advise against the often recommended feeding of poor-quality hay in addition to young pasturage, since the goats will eat too little of it for their roughage requirements. Besides, the energy deficit is only increased by such nutrient-poor hay.

A few leafy branches, on the other hand, are strongly recommended.

When the pasture or the green feed is sufficient for the energy and roughage requirements, no additional concentrated feed is necessary and is even not recommended, since otherwise the goat will eat too little basic feed. You should provide the goat with as much straw as it wants, preferably in a hay rack.

Constant access to a lick is particularly important for your goats at this time!

Fall

Because the growth of feed declines sharply in late summer (in dry years even earlier), it is good to be able to offer your goats additional feed from the fields or from the garden during this period.

Typical Daily Feed Ration in the Fall

Pasture/field fodder	6.6 lb (3.0 kg)
Beet greens, sunflower leaves, corn leaves	6.6 lb (3.0 kg)
Garden waste	1.1 lb (0.5 kg)
Concentrated feed	1.1 lb (0.5 kg)
Barley straw	as wanted
Fresh branches	small supplements

Typical Daily Feed Ration in Winter

Turnips	4.4 lb (2.0 kg)
Carrots	1.1 lb (0.5 kg)
Vegetable waste, fresh	1.1 lb (0.5 kg)
Hay	3.3 lb (1.5 kg)
Barley straw	as wanted
Concentrated feed	0.0–1.1 lb (0.0–0.5 kg)
Dried leafy branches and fresh evergreen branches	small supplements

Now, the concentrated feed no longer provides only the energy requirements but serves also to replenish protein. The following mixture has proven effective:

40 percent wheat bran
40 percent hulled oats
20 percent soy meal

In addition, also mix in (according to the directions on the package) a mineral feed and, if necessary, an herb mixture.

You can also buy an appropriate ready-mixed concentrated feed that is generally sold in feed stores as feed supplement for milk cows. Since, even with the best feeding, milk production declines in the fall, if you have sufficient basic fodder you don't need more than 1.1 pounds (0.5 kg) of concentrated feed per goat per day.

Winter

As a rule, the basis of winter feed is hay, of which an adult goat eats 2.2 to 4.4 pounds (1 to 2 kg) daily. In addition, you can feed turnips, carrots, potatoes, and fruit residues as they are available. You can feed potatoes raw (like carrots and beets), whole or cut up, but in any case well cleaned. One goat will eat about 6.6 pounds (3.0 kg) of these daily. The concentrated food requirements decrease with the decrease in milk production, or cease entirely if you let the goat remain dry.

In the six- to eight-week dry period before kidding, the goat should put on weight but not become fat. Not until one to two weeks before the birth do you again feed her a small handful of energy food. You should increase this quantity a little from day to day until by the day of birth you reach a level of about 1 pound (0.5 kg) of concentrated food per day. This way the rumen can slowly accommodate itself.

The birth of kids and with it the beginning of lactation usually occurs during the winter feeding period. After the birth you slowly increase the concentrated food portion, until no increase of the daily milk production is observable. You should not feed more than 2.21 pounds (1 kg) of concentrated food daily, because then too much basic feed will be crowded out of the ration.

The transition from winter feed to spring feeding is the most difficult situation of the year. Avoid an abrupt change of feed, and replace the winter feed with the young green fodder only in small steps, or allow the goats out into the pasture only for an hour at first. Watch the energy and roughage balance.

Pasturing and Stable Feeding

The pasture should be so divided among the goats that they always have fresh growth to eat, don't trample too much fodder, and crop the field as clean as possible. You can arrange such a controlled division either by tethering or by dividing the field into many individual well-fenced paddocks or by using a movable electric fence. A strong external fence all around the field, combined with an interior movable electric fence, is a more practical arrangement than are too many permanent internal fences, since they hinder mowing for care of the pasture and for haymaking.

The tether permits an exact division of the field but is quite labor-intensive and therefore suitable only for small herds. If you tether, you must be careful that the goats have enough distance from each other and cannot get entangled in each other's tether chains or ropes. The chains can also get wound around obstacles—tree stumps, for exam-

When they're indoors, goats are fed concentrate food.

ple. Since this problem cannot be avoided, despite all care, you should always keep your eye on your tethered goats or at least check every hour to see that all is well. Very often, one wants to make the tether chain or rope rather long, but this is very easily entangled. A short chain or rope, on the other hand, will always be kept tight and is therefore less likely to get wound around obstacles or the tethering post.

Guarding is also well-tolerated by goats. The use of guard dogs has proven to be effective, although the dogs trained as sheep herders must always adapt to some extent. Goats do not so easily allow themselves to

A pair of goats is tethered in a rice field.

Then they will not eat a single spot bare but will graze at random on the grain plants all over the whole field and will primarily seek out the weeds. Thistles and hedge mustard, especially, will be grazed out of the grain field this way.

Stable Feeding

You must bring in fresh green fodder for stable feeding daily. If you store it, spread it out loosely in thin layers; otherwise it will quickly get hot and can lead to dangerous bloating of the goats. Fodder that is rich in clover or damp is particularly dangerous. Feed that is mowed when damp picks up dirt very easily and then the goats don't like to eat it. Therefore, in spring and summer it is a good idea to keep a reserve of hay that can be fed on rainy days.

When green feed is used, the feeding shelf must be carefully cleaned twice a day. With dry feed, a daily cleaning is usually enough. Dirty and fermented food remnants can produce digestive upsets in goats and at the very least spoil their appetites, even if the freshly laid-out food is perfect.

Feed Requirements

For one goat of 132 pounds (60 kg) in weight and a milk production of 1,764 pounds (800 kg) per year, you need about 0.37 acres (0.15 ha) of green pasture with average yield for summer feeding and production of hay for the winter. In addition, you

be intimidated and resist sometimes. Also the usual "grip" used by dogs with sheep can sometimes injure the goat more easily because they lack the coat of wool.

On hot days the field must be provided with shade and water.

Pasturing with Other
Domestic Animals

Because of the different grazing habits, allowing goats to feed with other domestic animals—sheep, cattle, and even horses—is recommended. For one thing, the field will be better utilized overall than if it were used by just one type of animal. For another, the goats prevent invasive pasture weeds such as dock from spreading too much.

Grazing in the Cultivated Field

Before you drive your goats to the field to graze among grain crops, you must make sure that their hunger is already partially satisfied.

must figure some 551 pounds (250 kg) of concentrated feed yearly. These quantities will be smaller if you have available such supplementary feed as beets, potatoes, and so forth.

For hay storage, for about 1,102 pounds (500 kg) per goat, you need an area of 11.14 cubic yards (8.5 m^3) for loose storage and 6.55 cubic yards (5 m^3) for pressed bales.

If you raise kids only until weaning, the roughage requirement is just slightly increased. If, however, you are raising does for breeding, you must figure on an additional green pasture requirement per young goat per year of 0.12 acres (0.05 ha) and additional hay storage space of 3.9 or 2.2 acres (3.0 or 1.7 ha), depending on whether the hay is loose or baled.

Feeding Without Pasturage

If you do not have pasturage for your goats, you will need some 9.17 cubic yards (7 m^3) of storage space per goat for the yearly quantity of hay used as basic feed. This is based on the requirement of 4.4 pounds (2 kg) per goat per day and a once-a-year purchase of hay in pressed bales. If you don't have this much storage space available, you may perhaps wish to feed the highest possible amount of concentrated feed. In fact, increasing the concentrated feed portion beyond the normal quantity for goats is quite possible; you just must give them enough time to get used to the change. Never feed less than 1

pound (0.5 kg) of hay per goat per day, however.

Also, consider carefully whether you actually want to give your goats so much concentrated feed, which might directly nourish human beings, at least in part (the grain portion). From the ecological point of view, the goat really has the duty to make use of the roughage-rich feed that is otherwise not directly usable by mankind.

Providing Minerals

Mix mineral meal that is sold for goats in with the concentrated feed. Also hang a mineral lick or loose mineral mix in the stable as well. If the goats always have free access to it, they will not develop mineral deficiencies. It may happen that a positively extravagant consumption of mineral materials develops, but it is harmless and in a small goat holding it does not involve much financial outlay.

Watering

The goat's daily drinking water need ranges between 2.0 and 10.6

Salt and mineral blocks should be hung in the stable.

Goats should be able to feed in a sheltered area in case of inclement weather.

quarts (2 and 10 L), depending on the moisture content of the feed and the milk yield. When insufficient amounts of water are provided, the food consumption quickly increases. Goats particularly like slightly warmed water. If you water them from a pail, let the water stand in the sun for a while or mix some warm water into it so that it is just tepid. Many goats also like a shot of cider vinegar in their drinking water. Avoid dirtying the water, however.

Poisonous Plants

In their native habitat, goats learn to avoid poisonous plants. However, they have no special sixth sense that will warn them away from these harmful shrubs every time. Indeed, goats are specifically endangered by strange plants just because of their pronounced curiosity. If goats escape the pasture and explore an ornamental garden or a park, the venture can have serious consequences, since, among the decorative plants especially, there are a number of poisonous species—in particular, oleander (*Nerium*), arborvitae (*Thuja*), golden chain (*Laburnum*), monkshood (*Aconitum*), and yew (*Taxus*). The danger of prussic acid poisoning from withered leaves of stone fruit trees (*Prunus* species) has already been pointed out.

Chapter Six

Care and Management

Always keep goats in a group. Keeping them in single stalls is not appropriate to their nature and, from a financial point of view, is much too expensive. Tethered goats are also not able to maintain enough social contact with the other goats in the herd.

Group Keeping

Ranking Order

Fights for dominance in a newly assembled group are entirely normal social behavior. As goat keeper, keep your nerve and allow the goats to work out these problems by themselves as much as possible. After two to three days at most, peace and quiet should return to the group. Nevertheless, in the beginning it is advisable to keep a close eye on the animals. For if, in the exceptional instance, a strong goat regularly harasses a weaker one and does not leave it alone—even though the weak one acknowledges the higher rank and withdraws into a corner—you must play the role of leader yourself and discipline the inconsiderate goat with a box on the ear. The aggressor will generally accept it.

Even in an established herd squabbles about ranking order do arise from time to time. With a suitable feeding gate you can keep the higher-ranking goats from harassing the lower-ranking ones during feeding. There must of course be room at the feeding shelf for every goat—fasten the goats in the feeding gate during feeding. They will quickly get used to it and even use the same feeding place each time.

You can keep horned and unhorned goats in the same herd. The unhorned goats are at a disadvantage in the ranking battles, of course, since they primarily use their foreheads for pushing, so many goats favor biting as well, in order to intimidate rivals.

Other Animals

Goats can be kept in a group with sheep and cattle without any problems. In the pasture, such a mixed herd is even an advantage.

In mixed herds of sheep and goats, the goats take over the

Goats that graze on low grass risk getting worm infestations.

leadership as a rule. Usually, it is even desirable; nevertheless, the sheep can also learn uncharacteristic behavior from the goats, as, for example, the gnawing of fruit trees.

Between horses and goats there quickly develops a cozy friendship. It can go so far that the goat simply must be kept in the box with the horse.

Single keeping is very hard on such a sociable animal, so that you must then provide the company yourself. Go walking with your goat; it will soon follow you like a dog.

Stabling

With the proper arrangement of the stable, you create the conditions in which the goats will feel comfortable and you will also lighten the work for yourself.

• *Ventilate* the stable well at all times. A sharpening odor of liquid ammonia and some condensation on the walls are signs of lack of fresh air. Be careful when opening doors and windows that there is no draft, however. Without drafts, even cold air is not harmful.

• *The manure mattress* in the open stable will always remain clean and dry if you daily strew a small quantity of straw over it. There are now automatic sprayers that spray every 15 minutes around the clock. These sprayers, which use two size D batteries, are approved for use in processing rooms. One sprayer can handle 6,000 cubic feet (170 m^3) of enclosed area but is somewhat less effective in the open.

• *Controlling the fly plague:* You should use insecticides in the goat stable only with extreme caution. Broad-surfaced sticky fly traps are not injurious to health. Lucky is the goat keeper in whose stable there are swallows nesting and keeping the fly numbers down.

• *Daily cleaning:* Make sure the stable is clean. This is obvious for the feeding shelf, but you should also keep the stable walks and the storage areas clean.

A wet cleaning is not necessary; it is enough if the floor is swept clean. Even if you remove the manure from a stable area, it is enough to sweep the area clean afterward. The exceptions are the mother–child and nurturing areas, which you must disinfect at least once a year after careful scrubbing. You can obtain a stable

A dwarf goat climbing on rough rock to wear down its hooves.

disinfectant in the store or from the veterinarian. Also, strewing the floor with burnt lime has a disinfectant effect.

In case your veterinarian is of the opinion that your whole stable needs to be disinfected because of an infection, he will tell you the correct one to use and how to do it.

Yearly whitewashing: Once a year clean the walls and ceiling of dirt, dust, and spider webs with a broom. Then whitewash these surfaces with a mixture made as follows:

Combine 8 to 10.6 gallons (30 to 40 L) of white lime with 13.25 gallons (50 L) of water. Mix well and leave standing for one day. Shortly before using the solution, add about 2 quarts (2 L) of sour milk. This mixture will cover 1,614 to 2,152 square feet (150 to 200 m^2).

If there is any danger to pasturing goats, an electronic fence and herding dogs are a good idea.

The stable windows should be washed at least once yearly; in summer they are simply left open. Of course, only a portion of the sunlight comes through even the cleanest windows. In particular, the ultraviolet light that is so important for the health of the kids will be screened out. Therefore, provide your goats with exercise in the fresh air and sunlight.

Mice: In a clean stable there are only a few vermin. There will always be mice, however, and you must be careful that they soon don't dance under your nose. A good mousing cat is the best remedy, but you shouldn't give it anything to eat except a saucer of milk during milking. Make sure that your stable cat is worked regularly and is immunized against rabies.

Pasturing

A sojourn in the pasture serves not only to nourish the goat but also to promote health. You must not overlook the fact, however, that pastured goats are particularly at risk for worm infestations. Only if you carefully observe the rules of pasture hygiene and worm prevention are pastured goats also especially healthy goats.

Shelter

Goats are, of course, always exposed to the inclemency of the weather in the pasture. If you cannot quickly get them back into the stable, you need a hut that will protect them from wind, rain, and strong sunshine.

Tethered Goats

Tethered goats should not be left alone too long. When it rains, you must get them under a roof. Also, they do not tolerate being in brilliant sunlight for too long. Therefore, in high summer it's best to tether the goats in the shadow of a tree during the midday hours.

Water

On hot summer days the goats in the field must be able to drink, though as a rule it will be enough if they have sufficient water to drink in the stable at night and also have access to a mineral lick. Goats that are in the pasture day and night need free access there to water and mineral licks.

Pasture Fencing

Since goats quickly discover the weak spots in a fence, you must check it regularly for wires that are loose or rusted through, and for posts that are not firm or are broken. You test the guarding capability of the electric fence by grasping it with your hand. If the shock is uncomfortable for you, simply hold a blade of grass to the wire; the shock is then only a weak one. If the fence has no current, it probably is grounded somewhere; usually, the cause is grass that is too high, which then must be removed.

A colored German Edel buck bleating in the pasture.

The Care of Pastures and Meadows

Since goats don't graze their pasture clean, it must always be cleaned up by mowing. Ideally, you should alternate use of pasturing and cuttings. When a portion of the field is grazed over, mow the next growth and save it for hay because of the potential danger of parasites. In spring, level the molehills thrown up during the winter.

Fertilizing: In the fall, it's time for fertilization with manure and manure water. Try to make as even an application of manure over the field as possible.

You can also fertilize with chemical fertilizer, but perhaps you are reluctant to do so because, as a self-sufficient farmer, you are skeptical of the high yield claimed or are basically against it. Nevertheless, in

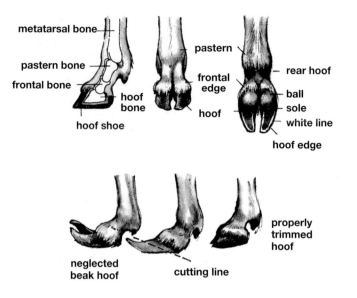

metatarsal bone

pastern bone

frontal bone

hoof shoe

hoof bone

pastern

frontal edge

hoof

rear hoof

ball

sole

white line

hoof edge

neglected beak hoof

cutting line

properly trimmed hoof

Goats have a very vigorous hoof growth because, in their natural setting, they climb on rocks; however, stable and grassy surfaces do not wear down hoofs. Therefore, hoofs must be trimmed regularly to prevent excessive growth.

case you do fertilize with it, try to promote the growth of weedy plants more than the grass in order to get a fodder consistent with the goats' tastes. For this purpose, phosphorus-rich fertilizers are good as an addition to manure from the stable. Chemical fertilizers with high nitrogen content are not usually suitable; this is especially true of ordinary commercial lawn fertilizers, which one-sidedly promote only the growth of grass. If you are in doubt, get the advice of an expert.

Skin Care

Goats are very agile at scratching themselves with the tips of their horns and their hoofs and by rubbing against posts and comers of walls. If they are not hindered in this skin care, if the stable is well ventilated,

and if they can also get into the sunlight regularly, there should be no problems with the skin, an important requirement for the well-being of the goat. In winter, especially when the goats are tethered in the shed, you should brush them regularly and hard with a cattle brush.

Hoof Care

The hoofs of the goat are particularly well adapted to its original habitat in the mountains. The hard wall of the hoof gives the goat a footing on small rock edges and steep turf slopes, while the soft ball clings to stone and rock surfaces. Of course, the hooves are well worn down on rough rock, but they grow back constantly.

On the other hand, in the domesticated goat, which mainly moves on the grassy surface of the field or on the straw in the stable, the hoofs grow far faster than they can be worn down. Consequently, they develop the so-called beaked hoofs and rolled hoofs. These produce a stress failure of the joint, which can ultimately lead to painful permanent injury. Dirt and foreign bodies also collect in these curled toes and can cause infections. Therefore, you must inspect and trim the hoofs regularly.

Hoof Trimming

Every six weeks you should examine the hoofs of your goats and, if necessary, trim them with a sharp pocketknife or pruning clippers.

- For kids, whose hoofs should be trimmed for the first time when the animals are six to eight weeks old, sit on a crate or a stool and take the kid between your knees.
- Press it onto its backside and hold its head in your lap. In this position you are directly facing the underside of the kid's outstretched hoof.
- First clean the hoof thoroughly of all dirt. Then with the knife or the clippers shorten the superfluous and perhaps already rolled-under hoof wall until it is even with the sole.
- Adult goats are better left standing during the hoof trimming, since it demands some strength to place the goat on its rear end. Tie the goat to a wall and press it against the wall. Now you can lift up the foot so that the sole is turned up, and proceed as just described.

If the hoof is already severely deformed by inadequate care, it is

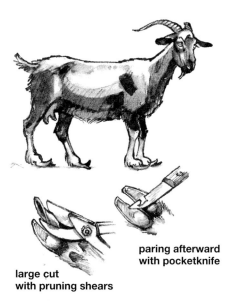

paring afterward
with pocketknife

large cut
with pruning shears

Goat hoofs can be trimmed with a sharp pocket knife. If the knife slips, though, the goat can be injured; therefore, it is better to use pruners.

This photograph shows typical hoof trimmers.

advisable to divide the trimming into several sessions, since otherwise the living tissue may be injured by a single drastic cut. Should a cut nevertheless penetrate the "living" tissue, paint the bleeding place with pine tar. You should always have enough light for your work on the hoofs.

Chapter Seven

Health Maintenance and Sickness

Healthy and Sick Goats

Goats are considered to be not very susceptible to illness. But, in large part, you determine this by proper maintenance, feeding, and care, which strengthen the goat's resistance and prevent the development of illness. You can create the conditions for the good health of your goats by providing
• feed in proper amounts and composition
• hygienic surroundings: clean stables, clean feed, and clean drinking water
• airy but draft-free, dry stable climate
• regular exercise of the goats
• parasite prevention
• regular skin and hoof care
• careful observation daily
• proper vaccination.

Under such conditions, sickness is rare among adult goats. Kids, on the other hand, are more susceptible, since their bodies must first learn to come to terms with the stresses of the environment. A healthy goat

• eats well
• chews its cud
• is lively, alert, and sociable
• has a smooth, shining coat (in pastured goats, as well as goats kept in a cold stable, the coat is often somewhat shaggy)
• walks and jumps without difficulty
• is well nourished but not fat
• has clear, clean eyes
• has a cool, dry nose
• has well-perfused mucous membranes
• drops dung in firm little balls
• has bright brown, clean urine
• has a normal body temperature of around 102.2° to 104°F (39° to 40°C) and a pulse of 40 to 80 beats per minute (somewhat more for kids).

Basically, goats can get sick just as any other farm animal can. Unfortunately, they are not immune to tumors and tuberculosis either, even if the latter is rarely reported. A goat that does not feel well or is really sick
• does not eat
• does not chew cud, and rumen shows no movement
• is bloated

Goat feed should be placed in feeders in order to prevent parasite infestations.

- goes off by itself and lies down a great deal
- has too low or too high a body temperature.

Further sure signs are
- diarrhea (if diarrhea is only intermittent, so that it is not always easily confirmed, it will be indicated by dried pieces of dung on the tail itself and just below it)
- blood in the urine
- not putting weight on one leg
- limping
- swollen joints
- pale mucous membranes
- discharge from muzzle and nose
- runny eyes
- rough coat, bristling coat, falling hair
- swollen body
- arched back
- malnutrition.

Treatments

For many ailments, you can undertake only a few appropriate procedures yourself and will require the technical skill of a veterinarian. Unfortunately, there are not many veterinarians with experience in the treatment of goats. It's best if you let the other goat keepers in your area recommend a veterinarian. When he or she arrives, inform him or her calmly of the details of the case and let the veterinarian explain how you might possibly have been able to prevent the illness.

As a rule, with good treatment, the goat surmounts small indispositions quickly. But if it is seriously ill, it is often a bad patient, because it appears—according to our human view—to quickly give up hope of recovery. The goat will refuse feed and lie there apathetically. It is therefore important that you give sick goats intensive care, talk with them a great deal, stroke them, feed them treats, and, as it were, build up their morale again with your sympathy. With these animals particularly, this is an important factor in recovery.

Keeping the Goats Healthy

While the livestock auction market provides a needed service in allowing farmers to sell or buy goats, it is also a place where infectious diseases and pests can be spread. Even if the animals arrive at the auction in good health, they will be exposed to many diseases that may cause sickness and death in your goats after arriving at home. Remember that infectious diseases have an incubation period, so it may be a while before the effects of exposure at the market are seen.

The goats can contaminate other stock already at your farm. Quarantine the new goats and prohibit fence-line contact for a period of 30 to 60 days. During the quarantine, vaccinate the new animals for enterotoxemia (overeating disease) and tetanus, and treat for both internal and external parasites. Other diseases that you should observe them for are pinkeye and respiratory diseases, which are associated with the stress of the sale.

To deal with basic goat health problems, consult your local veterinarian, because many of the medicines you may need to use are not approved for use on goats, unless prescribed by a licensed veterinarian. It is important to know that dosages recommended for sheep or cattle may not work for goats—too much or too little. Always read the labels and instructions carefully and follow the directions for using and storing medications. Specifically observe the withholding periods for meat and milk before human consumption. Put together a goat first aid kit with essential items for routine needs.

Internal Parasites

Cause

Practically all goats, even healthy and productive animals, harbor internal parasites. These are primarily various types of worms, which can live in the stomach and intestine, the liver, and the lungs of the goat. Their eggs are excreted with the goat's dung. These eggs develop directly or in an intermediate host—such as snails, for example—into infectious larvae, which are ingested by the goat with its fodder and develop in its insides into worms ready to reproduce.

Compared with other domestic animals, goats become especially burdened with these parasites. This disadvantage may be explained by the fact that in their original habitat they ate everywhere, especially from bushes and trees, where the danger of contamination of the feed with dung and of the possibility of intake of parasite larvae was limited. Therefore, perhaps, goats may have adapted less to internal parasites than some of the other plant eaters have.

Young goats are especially at risk of worms. Adult goats first become sick when their general condition worsens and, consequently, these interior parasites are able to reproduce vigorously. In this respect, undernourished goats are particularly susceptible, with the possibility that a deficit of even a single nutrient may unleash the illness. If there is a deficiency of minerals and vitamins in the feed, the combined effect is extraordinarily bad. Atmospheric conditions, too, especially heat and bad air in the stable, can add to the goat's diminished resistance to worms.

Coccidia are single-celled intestinal parasites, which practically all goats have. In otherwise healthy goats, they produce no injury as a rule. In kids, on the other hand, they can lead to intestinal illness resulting in death.

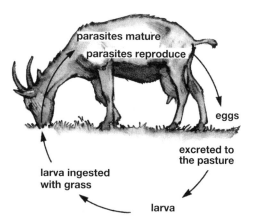

The goat itself is the source of ever-recurring infection with internal parasites. Unless this cycle is interrupted by the use of hygienic procedures in both stable and pasture, control with medications will have little chance of success.

Signs of Illness

Goats seriously affected with parasites lose weight, and the coat becomes rough. The mucous membranes of the eye and mouth become pale with anemia. The milk production falls off, and diarrhea occurs again and again. Frequently, the goats arch their backs, and edema under the jaw can occur. When lung worms are present, the goats can also have a nasal discharge and a cough, in addition to bad general condition.

A diagnosis of worms is established by the eggs, which the veterinarian detects in the feces.

If the meningeal worms are established in the brain, the goats will exhibit cramps and motor disturbances—especially compulsive circular movements. Death occurs after a few weeks.

Treatment and Prevention

Promote the goat's own resistance. Nourish the animal well and above all provide for a high mineral and vitamin content.

Stable and Pasture Hygiene

These are essential to prevention.
• Keep the intake of parasites to a minimum.

Goats that are allowed to climb on hay mounds may contaminate the hay with parasite eggs.

• Prevent fodder and drinking water from becoming fouled with dung.

• Clean the feeding shelf and the water containers regularly.

• As much as possible, provide fodder that is free of parasites. This is true of hay and leafy branches, for the most part.

• Collect green feed only from fields that have not been used as goat pastures or been fertilized with goat dung in the same year.

• Make sure that the litter straw is clean. A run should have a firm surface—of concrete blocks, for example—that is easy to keep clean.

• In pasture management, make sure that after an area is grazed over it is allowed to rest for at least three to six months. Even after this period, especially in humid weather, large numbers of infectious larvae may still be present. It is very good if the use of the field for pasture can be alternated with its use for a hay field. It is also advantageous to always insert a grazing with cows and horses between grazings with goats, since these other animals have relatively no internal parasites in common with the goat.

• If you have a lot of pasture available, use the same area as goat pasture only every two years. During the resting years, you can graze cattle and horses on the pasture.

• Avoid swampy pastures. One of the parasitic worm species that attacks the goat, the large liver fluke, needs as intermediate host for its development a particular snail, which can live only in damp areas. Drain the pasture, or fence in the swampy places in the field.

• Keep pasture stocking rate at six to seven goats per acre.

Worming with Medications

These supplement stable and pasture hygiene measures should reduce the number of parasites to an amount that is tolerable for the goat. A minimal number of worms not only is harmless but may, on the contrary, increase the goat's resistance.

Before each worming have the veterinarian examine a fecal sample of the goat, so that you will know the types of worm present and the extent of the worm infestation. Wormers such as Ivermectin, Moxidectin, Levamisole, Fenbendazole, and Albendazole have all been found effective. The majority of these wormers are well tolerated by goats but are not approved in some countries. Some of these medications should not be used during early or late pregnancy, since they can cause abortion. Ask your veterinarian for advice on proper wormers and the amount to be used, and find out which one is effective on your goat-raising condition.

Worming in the Rotating Pasture

If during the summer you regularly change pastures, either by means of tethering or by appropriate fencing, with at least three to six months of pasture rest period, you should need less worming. Experience has shown that the strategic time points at which the worms can be dealt with most effectively are
- the last month of pregnancy
- the day after kidding
- the beginning of spring and summer
- the end of the pasture season before returning the goat to the stable in the fall.

After the worming the pasture should be changed.

Worming in the Nonrotating Pasture

If your goats go from spring to fall in the same field, they should be checked and wormed regularly during this period. If at all possible, you should keep the goats in the stable for two days after the worming, so that they can unload the worm eggs there.

But it will always be difficult to keep the worms of goats under control in a nonrotating pasture, so that regular rotation of fields and as long a rest period for the pasture as possible are really the prerequisites for successful worm prevention.

Note: When goats are kept in the stable exclusively, worming is not necessary if feed and water can be kept from contamination.

Checking the Color of the Mucous Membrane of the Eye for Worm Monitoring

Wireworm (Barber's pole worm) is usually the biggest worm problem of the goats throughout the warm regions of the world, particularly in the subtropical and tropical areas. Major production losses and deaths can arise where the worm is not adequately controlled. As wireworms are bloodsuckers in the stomach, the effect of a heavy worm burden will therefore be evident by low blood cells. This is seen in mucous membranes of the eye as a visible paleness generally known as anemia. By monitoring anemia, resilient and susceptible goats can be identified.

Current recommendations include the worming of only animals in need, known as "selective treatment for worms." This can be decided by monitoring the color of the mucous membranes of the eye by use of the FAMACHA chart, which was developed in South Africa and validated in the United States. This consists of

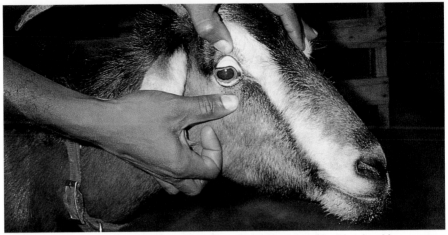

A pale mucous membrane of the eye is a sign of anemia caused by bloodsucking worms.

farmers examining the color of the lower eyelid of the goats, matching the color on the chart that ranges from red or healthy to almost white or anemic.

Digestive and Metabolic Disorders

Diarrhea

Cause
The goat responds quickly with diarrhea if too many mistakes occur in feeding—for example,
• with an abrupt change of one type of feed to another
• with too high an albumin content in the feed
• when the feed is frozen, fermented, or rotten

• if the proportion of concentrated food in the feed ration is too high.

But internal parasites can also produce diarrhea, and many infectious illnesses are accompanied by diarrhea.

A healthy intestine harbors many microorganisms without any difficulty for the goat. But if the resistance of the intestine is weakened by feed-generated diarrhea, which is harmless in itself, certain microorganisms in the intestine can reproduce unnaturally quickly and generate a reaction that produces sickness. A feed-related bacterial disease condition that causes almost sudden death is overeating disease (enterotoxemia). Under conditions of high carbohydrate feed consumption or high intake of immature forages, the bacteria multiply rapidly and produce a toxin causing diarrhea, depression, lack of coordination, and death.

Signs of Illness

In diarrhea caused by feed, the feces are brothy to liquid and the smell is usually quite noticeable. Watery, foul-smelling stool mixed with blood indicates an intestinal infection. If diarrhea alternates periodically with normal feces, you must suspect heavy worm infestation. If diarrhea persists for a long time, the goat loses weight and the coat becomes unkempt.

Treatment

Examine the feed for irregularities, withdraw the concentrated feed, and feed good hay and branches of fir, spruce, or pine. In most cases the feces will quickly become firm again with these measures. But there must always be enough fresh drinking water available. Withdrawal of water is harmful, since diarrhea leads to dehydration.

If the diarrhea persists, however, or keeps recurring, you must have a fecal sample examined for internal parasites.

If fluid diarrhea is mixed with blood or if the goat has fever along with the diarrhea, call the veterinarian.

With kids, diarrhea must be taken very seriously because it can quickly develop into a life-threatening illness.

Bloating

Cause

The gas that develops during digestion in the rumen can no longer be expelled by mouth because a foreign body—for example, a piece of apple—has blocked the esophagus. The goat swells up.

If the goat eats its fodder too hastily, doesn't produce enough saliva, or in an unsupervised moment gets into the concentrated feed sack and eats a great quantity of feed all at once, or if it eats too much damp clover or green feed that has grown warm in the stack, a foaming fermentation will occur in the rumen. The goat cannot belch up the gas-filled foam and will bloat.

Signs of Illness

The left flank bulges out in the area of the hunger cavity much more than on the right side. The goats have pain, gnash with their teeth, and strike out with their legs. Since the rumen also presses on the lungs, in serious cases respiratory failure can occur. This is a life-threatening ailment.

Treatment

You can usually feel a foreign body in the esophagus from outside and with some skill can massage it in the direction of the stomach. Otherwise, immediately remove the bloated goat from the feed and instill a foam-destroying preparation—for example, vegetable oil, or better, a silicon preparation (from the veterinarian), In light cases draw a string through the goat's mouth, on which it will chew, producing much saliva, which disperses the foam. You can also provide an outlet for the gas with a well-placed puncture through the puffed-up skin into the rumen with a special instrument, the trochar, or even simply with a pocketknife. In a foaming fermentation the relief for the goat remains minimal. Also, since infections can easily arise, you should try this last resort only if the goat threatens to die in spite of all other measures and if no veterinarian can be reached.

Prevention

Be sure that the goats do not eat too much young green fodder or clover in too short a time or do not rush hungry into a young pasture that is still wet with dew, or else always feed them some hay first. Stored green fodder should not be allowed to get warm.

Bloating of the belly of a suckling kid is a consequence of faulty milk digestion.

Acid Rumen

Cause

If a goat too quickly eats an unusually large quantity of easily digested starch- or sugar-rich food, such as bread, wheat, sugar beets, concentrated food, and so on, an excess of acid can develop in the rumen.

Signs of Illness

The goat is apathetic, its head droops, and it acts somewhat as if it were drunk. It can also bloat.

Treatment and Prevention

The goat should be separated from the feed immediately but provided with plenty of drinking water. If it can't get up and keeps lying there,

the situation is life threatening. In this case, call the veterinarian at once.

An excess of rumen acid can be avoided if you accustom the goat slowly, in increasing quantities, to easily digested feed. Store the concentrated feed so that the goats can't help themselves to it.

Ketosis

Cause

In good milk goats, when the milk production occurring after birth increases rapidly, the necessary energy for this usually cannot be completely provided by the feed that is ingested. Therefore, the goat must draw on body reserves. The breakdown of fat produces so-called ketone bodies, which in large quantities have the effect of poison.

Signs of Illness

Food intake and milk production fall off, the coat becomes rough, the goat is apathetic. Breath, urine, and milk have a sweetish odor. Severely ill goats lie down and fall into a fatal coma.

Treatment and Prevention

The veterinarian usually provides effective help.

In the weeks after birth, milk goats must take in as much energy as possible. Accustom them slowly to the necessary quantity of concentrated food by beginning about two weeks before the kidding date with a small handful of food and then gradually increasing the daily feeding so

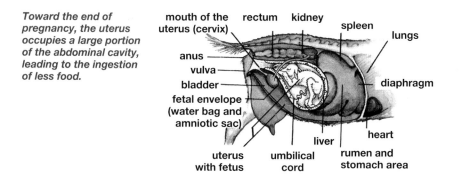

Toward the end of pregnancy, the uterus occupies a large portion of the abdominal cavity, leading to the ingestion of less food.

Labels in diagram: mouth of the uterus (cervix), rectum, kidney, spleen, lungs, anus, vulva, bladder, fetal envelope (water bag and amniotic sac), diaphragm, uterus with fetus, umbilical cord, liver, rumen and stomach area, heart

that by the day of the birth you have reached about 1.10 pounds (0.5 kg). Give the daily ration of concentrated feed in the smallest possible portions. The basic fodder should be of the best quality to achieve the highest feed intake possible.

Pregnancy Toxemia

Cause

This is a condition similar to ketosis and can arise in the end phase of pregnancy. In this period, especially in the case of twin or even triple births, the energy requirement for the development of the kids is very great. At the same time, the ever-increasing uterus takes space from the rumen, and the mother goat is thus able to eat less and less. She is forced to draw on her body reserves, and in the breakdown of body fat the ketone bodies develop in large, poisonous quantities.

Signs of Illness

Ailing goats no longer eat, appear blind, and can quickly fall into a fatal coma.

Treatment and Prevention

Unfortunately, in contrast to ketosis, the veterinarian is often not able to do much. Feed the best possible quality roughage during the last weeks of pregnancy. You should increase the concentrated feed portion only during the last two weeks, however.

Because fat goats are especially at risk of ketosis as well as of toxemic pregnancy, it is better to keep milk goats somewhat thin, particularly in the second half of the lactation period, and not allow them to consume too much concentrated food during the dry period. Goats that are able to exercise freely are less susceptible to these disorders.

Milk Fever

Cause

With the onset of milk production after birth, the goat loses a large quantity of calcium with the milk. Of course, each goat normally has enough calcium reserves in her bones, but she can have "forgotten" during pregnancy to mobilize these reserves, since then the calcium requirement is smaller. The goat forgets it especially quickly if in this period the feed is very rich in calcium—for instance, if the feed is alfalfa or the concentrated feed has a high calcium content.

Signs of Illness

Before the kids are born, the goat displays a weak, limping gait. In serious cases, she lies unmoving after the birth and can sink into a coma.

Treatment and Prevention

Call the veterinarian at once, who can help quickly, even in acute cases, with an infusion of calcium.

Toward the end of pregnancy, be careful not to use a feed too high in calcium; especially, feed little alfalfa or alfalfa hay. Have your feed tested for the calcium-phosphorus content and, in case of a notable excess of calcium, regulate it by supplementing with a phosphorus-rich mineral feed with a ratio of 1.5:1 to 2:1.

Colds

Cause

In drafts and damp cold, goats can easily become ill with inflammations of the respiratory system. The sickness is promoted by a high content of injurious gases in the air, especially ammonia, which is produced by the breakdown of dung and urine. Cold by itself does no harm.

Signs of Illness

Goats that have caught cold breathe hard, have a nasal discharge, and sneeze or cough. They eat with little appetite and have fever.

Treatment and Prevention

The illness can be tiresome and difficult to treat, even with the help of a veterinarian, so it's a good prevention measure to make sure that the stable is draft free but well ventilated. The resting area must be dry and warm. In winter it is better for the stable to be cold and dry than warm and damp. In severe cold you must go out of your way to avoid burdening the goat with a change of feed or a change of stabling.

Udder Inflammation (Mastitis)

Cause

The udder, a high-performance organ, can be attacked by a whole string of infectious illnesses. The most important of them are the various forms of udder inflammation, in which milking plays a definite developmental role. Most often, the inflammations are caused by microorganisms, mainly bacteria, which enter the interior of the udder through the teat. This entry usually takes place directly after milking, when the udder is empty. The infectious agents, or pathogens, are present everywhere in the environment of the goat. Less often, the pathogens from other body areas enter the udder through the bloodstream.

The tissue of the interior of the udder is ordinarily able to protect itself against invasive infectious agents. But if it is impaired and if the pathogens are produced in great quantities, an inflammation may result. Injuries to the udder tissue are a consequence of poor milking technique to begin with. Bruising and stretching are the faults in hand milking; too high a vacuum, wrong rhythm cycle, and blind milking (after the udder is already empty) are the faults in machine milking. Furthermore, with machine milking there is increased risk of the direct transmission of infection from goat to goat by the milking machine itself.

Signs of Illness

Since both halves of a goat's udder are completely separate systems from one another, frequently only one half is affected by an inflammation. Differentiation is made between acute and chronic mastitis.

Acute mastitis—The affected half of the udder is painfully swollen, the milk production is strongly decreased, and the milk is usually flaky and tastes salty. The goat is visibly ill and has fever.

Chronic mastitis—The signs of illness are less obvious. Occasionally some coloration or flakes appear in the milk, and the affected udder half can be somewhat difficult to milk. The goat shows no general signs of illness. Have the veterinarian show you a quick test you can do yourself—for example, the California Mastitis Test (CMT) or the

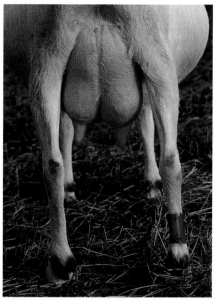

A goat with udder inflammation.

Somatic Cell Count (SCC). If you milk with a machine, you should perform such a test regularly on all milk goats.

Chronic mastitis greatly influences the milk production; the milk is badly tolerated by children and adults with sensitive stomachs and causes difficulties with the production of cheese.

Treatment and Prevention

Acute mastitis—Only the doctor can help. His or her prescription for the use of antibiotics should be followed exactly; it is essential that the prescribed dose not be reduced, even if the inflammation disappears quickly. It is equally important that the waiting time before the milk is used afterward be complied with

A goat with a CL abscess.

exactly, to avoid health problems for human beings as well as failures with cheese making. A salve that promotes circulation and aids in the treatment can be applied to the udder.

Chronic mastitis—This too must be treated with an antibiotic according to the veterinarian's instructions. A treatment with special long-term antibiotics, which are injected into the udder after the last milking before the dry period, is very helpful.

Because antibiotic treatments are expensive and their continuous use can induce infectious agents to develop resistance to them, and because not a few goat keepers also avoid the use of antibiotics on principle, the main effort in mastitis prevention must lie in clean and considerate milking.

Caseous Lymphadenitis (CL abscess)

Cause

This is a common infectious and rapidly transmittable disease of sheep and goats caused by bacteria that result in abscesses in lymph nodes. The bacterium enters the goats' body through small breaks in the skin and eventually becomes localized in lymph nodes.

Signs of Illness

Most common lymph nodes affected are the ones below the ears, lower jaw, in front of the shoulder, and in front of the rear knee joint. The abscessed lymph nodes are swollen and may rupture and drain greenish pus that contaminates the herdmates and the surroundings.

Treatment and Prevention

There is no effective antibiotic therapy for CL abscess. The goat should immediately be isolated and veterinary advice sought. Affected animals may have to be culled to prevent transmission of the disease to the other herdmates.

Polioencephalomalacia (PEM)

Cause

PEM (thiamine deficiency) is most commonly seen in kids two to six months old that are fed a high-concentrate diet. However, PEM can be seen in animals of any age. Sudden change in diet, feed high in molasses (horse feed), and moldy hay can trigger the disease. In ruminant animals, the digestive bacteria normally produce enough thiamine (Vitamin B_1), but diets high in grain and low in forages can result in depressed production of thiamine.

Signs of Illness

Ailing goats show blindness, depression, incoordination, head pressing, and convulsions. Severly sick goats can become comatose and die.

Treatment and Prevention

Therapy must be started by a veterinarian early in this disease to be effective. Treatment of choice regardless of the cause is giving thiamine injections. Response is dramatic and almost immediate. The diet should also be modified to reduce grain and increase forage intake. During times of stress, or when predisposing diets are unavoidable, the inclusion of the thiamine in the feed may aid in prevention.

Pinkeye

Cause

Pinkeye is an eye infection caused by bacteria. The disease is usually sudden and tends to spread rapidly. One or both eyes may be affected. Dry, dusty conditions, bright sunlight, flies, and tall grasses tend to predispose to the problem.

Signs of Illness

The initial signs are closure of the eye, increased tearing followed by inflammation and varying degree of cornea cloudiness, and ulcer, which may lead to temporary blindness.

Treatment and Prevention

Good management is important in reducing or preventing the spread

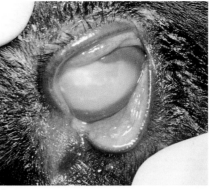

Cornea cloudiness indicates a case of pinkeye.

of infection. Affected goats need to be separated to prevent further spread and treated by topical eye antibiotic ointments. If topical therapy is not practical, injection of long-acting antibiotics may be ordered by your veterinarian. Temporary isolation of newly introduced goats to the herd may be helpful to prevent introduction of the disease to your herd since some animals may carry the bug and not show the disease.

Gait Problems

Joint Disorders

Cause

Rheumatic illnesses occur frequently in damp, cold environments. Little is known about the cause. For one particular form only, caprine arthritis encephalitis (CAE), a virus, is known to be the agent. The transmission presumably goes primarily

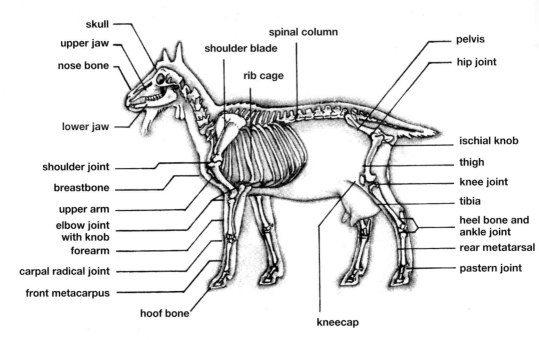

The goat's skeleton.

Labels (clockwise from top left): skull, upper jaw, nose bone, lower jaw, shoulder joint, breastbone, upper arm, elbow joint with knob, forearm, carpal radical joint, front metacarpus, hoof bone, kneecap, spinal column, shoulder blade, rib cage, pelvis, hip joint, ischial knob, thigh, knee joint, tibia, heel bone and ankle joint, rear metatarsal, pastern joint

from mother to kid through the beastings (colostrum), that is to say, through the first milk the mother provides after birth. Infection of an adult goat appears to be rare but cannot be ruled out.

Signs of Illness

The area of the joint is severely swollen. In the beginning the ability to move is often not much affected, though the disorder usually turns out to be chronic. The goat's difficulty moving increases continually, and the pain finally becomes so bad that the goat lies down. Besides chronic inflammation of the joints, CAE can also produce changes in the udder,

similar to the appearance of an udder inflammation. Since the virus develops very slowly, affected goats can excrete it for a year before the appearance of joint difficulties, which allow diagnosis of disease. Blood tests enable us to identify these goats. Cerebral meningitis can occur in kids affected with CAE virus.

Treatment

Pain can be lessened by applying salves that increase circulation; the goat will be able to move for a while longer. Warmth also helps to decrease the pain. But in the long run, there is practically no hope of healing for chronic joint ailments.

Even with CAE, though the virus can be identified, there is at present no available treatment with medication or an immunizing shot.

Some goat breeders try to combat this disease by excluding animals identified as carriers from further breeding or by separating the kids from the mother at birth and feeding them the colostrum of healthy goats or cows. If such colostrum is not at hand, the colostrum of the ailing mother can be cleansed of the CAE virus without losing too much of the colostrum's special quality by heating it at 131°F (55°C) for 60 minutes.

Foot Rot

Cause

This hoof inflammation is brought about by bacteria, which are easily passed from goat to goat. Sheep suffer more than goats from foot rot, and the infection of goats is often caused by affected sheep. Humid weather and damp ground promote the infection.

Signs of Illness

The goats limp or only slip forward on bent legs because they have such severe pain in their hoofs. The hoofs are inflamed; in well advanced stages the hoof skin may even detach.

Treatment and Prevention

Get the advice of a veterinarian or an experienced shepherd. Trim and disinfect the hoofs under his direction. Foot rot in goats can definitely

be avoided with regular hoof care, dry pastures, and clean litter in the stable. If your goats have contact with sheep, make certain that these are free of hoof rot.

Skin Problems

Cause

Fungus and skin parasites, especially mites and lice, plague goats, particularly if they have little opportunity to groom their skin by rubbing, scratching, and licking. Therefore, these problems most often occur with goats tethered in a stable.

Signs of Illness

The skin jumps noticeably, for the goat tries to scratch itself in all possible ways. Hair falls out, and scales, crusts, or bald spots develop on the skin.

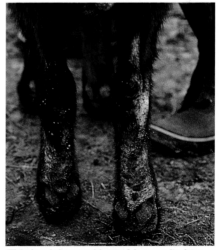

This buck has a skin problem on its legs.

Basic Goat Vaccination Needs

• A minimal vaccination for goats consists of vaccines against overeating disease (enterotoxemia) and tetanus. A combined vaccine is available in many countries for these two common goat diseases.

• All the animals should be vaccinated initially and receive a second vaccination in three to four weeks.

• Pregnant goats should receive their yearly vaccination one month before giving birth. Bucks, yearlings, and other adults should also receive a yearly vaccination.

• Goats that are fed large amounts of concentrate feed may need to receive a vaccination every six months.

• Kids should initially receive two injections of the vaccine three to four weeks apart at one or two months of age and yearly vaccinations afterward. Ask your veterinarian for specifics and brand of vaccine.

Treatment and Prevention

Treat the affected goat quickly and on the advice of the veterinarian to prevent infection of other animals.

A healthy skin with good blood circulation is not so easily afflicted with fungus and parasites. Goats in an open stable and in the pasture have enough chance to lick themselves or each other, to scratch themselves—horned goats have the advantage here!—or to rub against posts and walls. Fresh air and sunshine promote the skin's ability to resist. In the tethered stable you must regularly brush the goats hard with a stiff cattle brush.

Wounds

Disinfect wounds with tincture of iodine or paint them with pine tar. You can also order a special wound spray from the veterinarian. Gaping wounds must be stitched by the veterinarian. Wash inflamed and suppurating wounds or bathe them with chamomile tea. For abscesses, apply scarlet dressing, icthyol ointment, or a similar wound dressing. A fly-repellent powder may also be dusted over the area to keep it free from flies and bacteria. Reapply the powder as necessary.

Tetanus cannot be prevented by wound disinfection alone. In areas where the disease is prevalent, precautionary immunization is recommended. Ask your veterinarian.

Goat Diseases That Endanger Humans

Some goat illnesses can also be transmitted to humans if they come into close contact with the animals themselves or with their products.

Rabies

Pastured goats can get rabies if they are bitten by a rabid animal. The rabies virus produces disorder of the brain, which is expressed in numerous forms of abnormal behavior but need not necessarily be accompanied by aggressiveness. Transmission of the virus can occur only through wounds. Since the infection of humans with rabies is always life threatening, you should call the veterinarian at once at the least suspicion of rabies and let him or her decide about further measures.

A precautionary immunizing shot is available for humans and animals.

Toxoplasmosis

This is a disease of cats produced by a protozoa. The microbe can also cause abortion in goats. The signs of illness in the goat are so minor that as a rule they are overlooked. Of course, the microbes will be excreted with the milk and can produce severe injury to fetuses and infants drinking raw milk. Therefore, goat milk should be pasteurized or boiled before human consumption.

Tuberculosis

In goats, tuberculosis can arise in different organs. The transmission to human beings is accomplished through the milk. Fortunately, tuberculosis is eliminated in the domestic animals in most countries today by strict preventive measures.

Brucellosis

In Europe brucellosis has also been largely eliminated, but in the Mediterranean and in many countries of the tropics and subtropics it is still widespread. It is transmitted by bacteria and can produce abortion in the goat. The infectious agent can also be transmitted to human beings through the milk and can produce the often-protracted undulant fever. Frequently, the goats excrete the bacteria without themselves exhibiting any notable signs of illness.

Caution: Unless the possibility of transmission of illness through milk is definitely ruled out, the milk should be boiled or pasteurized before using, that is, heated to 185°F (85°C) or heated for 40 seconds at 159.8° to 165.2°F (71° to 74°C). The agents of infection will also be killed by the long ripening to hard cheese, but this is not the case with fresh cheese.

If you want to be entirely certain, have your milk tested regularly for infectious agents by a veterinary testing agency. Your veterinarian can tell you the appropriate agency.

Chlamydia

Chlamydia is the most common cause of abortion in goats in the United States and is present in other countries as well. Goats can miscarry in any stage of pregnancy, but most are common in the last month. This disease is readily transmittable to human beings from animals. During kidding season, pregnant women assisting with birthing may become infected and miscarry. Therefore, they should avoid contact with the herd during kidding season

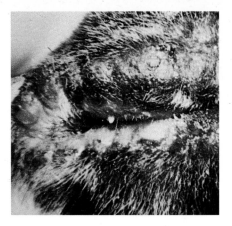

Sore-Mouth (Orf)

Sore-Mouth is a disease of sheep and goats caused by a virus causing blisters on the nose and lips of young animals. Humans are occasionally affected by touching the blisters or scabs when handling the goats. Goat handlers should exercise care and wear gloves when handling goats with blisters and crusts around the mouth.

and wear masks and latex gloves if they have to work with the goats during their pregnancy.

Q Fever

This is a disease that affects a variety of animals as well as humans. It can cause abortion in sheep and goats and has been reported in North America and elsewhere. Cows are a source of infection for goats when they share pastures and feed source. Humans can get the infection by inhalation of contaminated dust, contact with aborted material and while assisting in birthing, and consumption of unpasteurized milk. The disease in human beings is characterized by influenza-like symptoms. Goat milk should be pasteurized or boiled before human consumption. All persons should wear masks and gloves when removing manure from the barn and when assisting with kidding.

The Small Stable Pharmacy

You should be prepared to treat simple ailments and wounds as well as to administer first aid until the veterinarian comes. You should have on hand
• a fever thermometer
• bandaging material, adhesive tape, and large sterile gauze pads
• pine tar
• 2 percent tincture of iodine or wound spray
• icthyol ointment, scarlet dressing, or similar wound dressing
• diarrhea medications (charcoal or oak bark powder)
• 10-ml syringe and several 18-gauge hypodermic needles stored in a sterile jar.

Chapter Eight

Breeding and Raising Young

Estrus and the Reproductive Cycle

A goat in estrus is conspicuously restless, bleats constantly, and wags her tail. She tries to mount other does and allows them to mount her. The vulva swells, usually becomes red, and mucus may appear, which toward the end of estrus becomes yellowish and cloudy. At the peak of estrus the goat is ready to mate and tolerates mounting by the buck.

These manifestations are the outer signs that the ovary of the goat has a fertile egg in readiness and the uterus is ready to allow the fertile egg to establish itself.

If a female goat is not bred or does not become pregnant, she "comes into heat" at regular intervals, as the onset of the manifestations of estrus is termed. This regularly repeated occurrence is described as the reproductive cycle. Its length, that is, the interval between one heat and the next, usually amounts to three weeks; thus one figures with a variation of about 17 to 23 days. Sometimes a very short cycle that may last only a week can be observed in very young goats.

Hormones govern the menstrual cycle, whose principal control resides in the brain. Therefore, the reproductive cycle does not always run the same mechanically; it is influenced by sensory impressions such as sight, smell, hearing, and feeling, which are processed in the brain.

Seasonal Limitation of Estrus

In goats the onset of estrus is almost exclusively seasonal; that is, it only occurs at a particular time of year. This has a basis in nature: for the wild ancestors of our domesticated goats, mating in spring and summer meant that they must then raise the resulting kids in winter, a situation that would have meant almost certain death. Kids from fall and winter breeding, on the other hand, grow in the climactically favorable and plentiful feeding periods of spring and summer. In European areas, the breeding season begins in the second half of the month of August, continues deep into the winter, and ends again in January to February. The light of the increasingly longer days of spring inhibits the goat's reproductive cycle. Only when the days become increasingly shorter after the summer sun turns away does estrus begin again. The repression of estrus by light is not always complete, so that you should not wonder if sometimes the goat comes into heat outside the normal breeding season. There are also other influences that can strengthen or diminish the blockade effect of the light.

• The presence or the smell of a buck can induce estrus.

• The same goes for the presence of other goats in heat.

• High temperatures can inhibit estrus, whereas lower ones may induce it. This is true not only for the first appearance of estrus at the beginning of the breeding season but also for the more or less strong expression of estrus during the breeding period.

In contrast to European/American goat breeds, the dwarf goats have not developed any particular seasonal reproductive rhythm in the conditions of their tropical habitat, and therefore they can be bred and can bear all year long in Europe and America.

The Boer goats again display a distinctly seasonal estrus, like that of European/American breeds.

Confirmation of Estrus

Usually it is not difficult to confirm estrus in goats, at least in those that have already kidded once, since the signs of estrus described at the beginning of this chapter appear very clearly. In young goats, on the other hand, the signs are not always so unequivocal. You can test by scratching and pressing the goat at the base of the tail. If she stops and lifts her tail, it is very probable that she is in heat. Otherwise, she would tuck her tail under and retreat to one side.

It is helpful to maintain a calendar on which you note the onset of estrus precisely for each goat so that you can then observe for the signs from time to time after about 18 days.

The approaching estrus will also be intensified if you rub a buck—preferably between the ears—with a burlap bag and thus carry his odor to the doe. Of course, actually bringing the doe together with the buck provides the very best diagnosis of estrus.

The Best Mating Time

The doe remains in heat for about 36 hours. Since the release of the egg occurs just at the end of the outward signs of estrus or immediately afterward, it is only

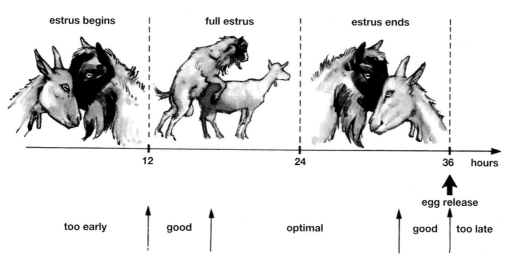

estrus begins	full estrus	estrus ends

```
                    12            24                    36   hours
                                                        ↑
                                                   egg release
     too early  ↑   good  ↑        optimal      ↑   good │ too late
```

The most favorable time for mating is about a day after the beginning of estrus.

then that the egg can be fertilized. If you bear in mind that the semen of the buck is also only fertile for a limited time, it will be clear that the best time for breeding is toward the end of estrus. Indeed, the goat can even be successfully fertilized at the end of the period, as long as the buck still succeeds at coition.

Breeding Age

Female and male goats are sexually mature from the age of four to five months. Therefore, if the kids are born in the spring, the sexual maturation coincides with the beginning of the breeding season in the fall. A normally developed young doe can be bred at the age of about nine months without problems and will kid for the first time at the age of 14 months. There is no sensible reason for first breeding young does in the succeeding season at the age of about 18 months.

Naturally, pregnant young does must be so well fed that not only the nutrient requirements for the pregnancy are met but also those for the body growth that is still continuing.

Occasionally, a mother goat will go into heat again a short time after kidding in late winter. Breeding at this time is usually not successful, because the goat's reproductive organs have not yet recovered enough. The milk goat's production will quickly fall off with a new pregnancy.

Hornlessness and Fertility

There is a direct relationship between hornlessness and fertility. Hornless goats either are themselves infertile, because of an androgynous development of the reproductive organs, or carry this trait even if they themselves are normally fertile. Hornless bucks can suffer from blocked semen and also carry the gene for the development of androgyny.

Horned goats are normally fertile.

If you don't want to give up the idea of hornless does, you should at least cover them with a homozygous horned buck. Then all the immediate offspring are normally fertile.

In mating season, bucks exhibit flehmen behavior when females are in heat nearby.

Buck Maintenance and Breeding

The Buck Smell

The reproductive behavior of bucks also shows seasonal variations. After the decline of the summer sun, they show increased interest in the does, and the proverbial billy goat smell becomes increasingly noticeable. This arises partly from the special scent glands located just behind the base of the buck's horns. In addition, during the mating season, the bucks have the custom of urinating into their mouths and sprinkling their breasts with the urine. This then contributes to the typical buck smell. Human beings usually perceive this odor as unpleasant; the keeper of billy goats is willing to put up with it, but it can really irritate neighbors. Cauterizing the scent glands can usually reduce the odor considerably, but some animal protection laws no longer permit such a practice without further examination. Ask your veterinarian. For transporting bucks during the breeding season, you had best use gloves and a coverall that is worn only in the buck stable, since the smell is difficult to get rid of even with careful washing.

Mounting

This odor has a very exciting effect on the doe. When a doe comes to a buck, he greets her with a bleating hu-hu and smells her from all sides, but especially in the tail region. If she is in heat, she will sometimes tolerate the rather rough caresses of the male. He smells or tastes her urine, also, after which he exhibits flehmen—that is, he draws up his upper lip with his head held high. Then he strikes the ground with his forefeet, lays them on the doe's shoulders, and tries to mount her. If the goat is at the peak of estrus, she tolerates the mounting and lifts her tail so that the buck can copulate. The successful conclusion of the mating act is recognizable by the powerful thrust in which the buck raises himself high.

If the first mating is properly carried out, immediate repetition has little point. But a second mating can be a good idea if the goat is still in heat 24 hours after the first one. A buck can mate about 10 to 20 times a day; you can figure that he can mate with about 50 goats altogether.

During the mating season, the bucks eat little and can lose a great deal of weight. If a buck is greatly in demand, you must feed him with enough concentrated feed; treats such as dried leafy branches do him good.

Toward the end of winter, the sexual urge of the buck declines increasingly but can still be aroused sometimes by contact with goats in heat. In spring and summer, he can of course mate in principle, but he has little desire to do so and few pregnancies result. He stops urinating in his mouth during this time. Thereafter, the billy goat smell will diminish considerably.

During the mating season, the buck urinates on his head and has a billy goat odor.

Keeping Bucks

In nature there are no malign bucks. They can, however, regard the human as a rival and challenge him to a battle for dominance. If the buck keeper meets this challenge quietly but forcefully, he will have no problem. However, strangers should approach the buck with appropriate caution. You should not even poke playfully at young breeding bucks, since they respond to this game just like adult bucks. Rather, show your affection by scratching them on the neck.

Naturally, the goat buck must also be healthy in order to be used for breeding without any problems; healthy legs and joints are especially important for this.

Artificial insemination is also possible with goats.

Pregnancy

The most important indication of pregnancy is the failure of the next heat to occur. Therefore, it is worthwhile to observe particularly carefully three weeks after the mating of the doe.

Pregnancy lasts about 150 days, with a variation range from 146 to 152 days. Multiple pregnancies, as a rule, are of somewhat shorter duration than single ones. Twin pregnancies are the most frequent, but not infrequently there are also triplets or quadruplets; however, goats that are themselves products of a single birth often bear only a single kid.

In the later stages of pregnancy, the young can often be felt through the wall of the abdomen. A test of hormones in the milk or in the blood can detect the pregnancy early and with certainty. At insemination stations such tests are carried out very reasonably. Ask your veterinarian. There is also ultrasound apparatus for determination of pregnancy. Using it successfully requires much experience and is not practical for the small-scale goat keeper.

As pregnancy progresses, the milk production continues to decline. To provide the udder with a recovery period, the goat is allowed to go dry about six to eight weeks before the birth date—that is, milking is stopped. You should milk for several days only once daily and then, after a last, careful milking, stop milking completely, if possible with the use of special antibiotics. The udder will swell at first, but this is entirely natural and it goes down after several days.

At the beginning of the dry phase, the goat should not be fed too richly; then later, you need to pay attention to the special feed requirements of the pregnant goat.

Birth

Even for an experienced goat keeper, the birth of kids is always a tense experience. When you are a novice and facing your first birthing, you are sure to be a little excited. During the birth, doubts will come to you again and again about whether everything is running smoothly.

Most goats give birth without difficulty and preferably without the presence of a human being, even if they otherwise have a trusting relationship with one. The supervision and support of a birth—in particular, the help in pulling—must therefore proceed very cautiously. Many birth difficulties can be induced when the impatient or uncertain goat keeper interferes in the natural birth process. The best birthing help for the goat is a good preparation through a diet that is not too rich and through enough exercise.

The normal course of a birth is described in the following sections. If you observe any marked departures from this, call the veterinarian, unless an experienced goat breeder is lending a helping hand.

Before the Birth

The impending birth is signaled by the obvious enlarging of the udder. The vulva swells, and the pelvic ligaments at the base of the tail relax. The goat is restless and excretes small quantities of dung and urine frequently. She trips in place, lies down, stands up again, and turns her head to her tail, while she often bleats softly.

Her herd companions take great interest in a delivering goat; if in their curiosity they come a bit too close, however, she waves them back with a threatening shake of her head, especially if she is lying down in a quiet corner in the end phase.

Therefore, do not take a goat about to give birth out of the herd. She will become so excited about the separation that the course of the birth will be disturbed. Only when the kids have come into the world will the mother gladly retreat with them into their own quarters.

During the Birth

In the uterus the fetus is enclosed in a sac of skin, the amniotic sac, which is surrounded by another sac of skin, the water bag. At birth the water bag appears first. It widens the birth canal gently and may occasionally be started prematurely; just as infrequently it may be followed by the amniotic sac.

Soon the water bag bursts and lets go a torrent of amniotic fluid. After that a normal birth can last for up to two hours longer. Usually the kid appears, wrapped in the amnion, with the front feet forward and the head lying on them; less often the hind feet appear first. Under the increasing pressure of labor, the amniotic sac also breaks finally, and the mucus from it acts as an excellent lubricant to help the expulsion of the kid. At the passage of the head, the birth slows, especially in goats bearing for the first time, to give the birth canal still more time to dilate. Once the head has fully emerged, after a short interval the body of the kid is completely expelled with some labor.

After the Birth

For a brief time the expelled kid lies there motionless. Then it lifts and shakes its head and tears the skin of the amniotic sac, which is still clinging to it.

It is necessary to help with freeing only very frail kids from the amniotic sac. The umbilical cord also breaks by itself, at the latest when the mother stands up.

Immediately after birth the mother begins licking the kid to free it of mucus and to stimulate its breathing. With very weak kids, you can draw off the external mucus from the mouth and nose and, by rubbing the skin with straw, can stimulate breathing. In any case, disinfect the stump of the umbilical cord with an antibiotic spray or with tincture of iodine. The goat will stop licking in order to expel other kids.

Soon the kids try to stand up and usually begin to suckle after a half

Barely into the world, the kid tries to stand on its feet. It is still a bit wobbly on its legs, but soon it will be up to nurse from its mother.

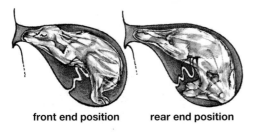

front end position   rear end position

Normal front and rear end birth positions.

hour. If the udder is very greatly swollen, they sometimes begin a little clumsily. Then you must help them a bit. The quick and ample intake of this first "beastmilk," also called colostrum, is of paramount importance for the kids. The sucking also promotes the expulsion of the afterbirth, which is completed within a few hours after the birth. The mother eats the afterbirth; this is a completely natural behavior and should not be interfered with. Retention of the afterbirth rarely occurs in goats. Should this happen, call the veterinarian.

Assisting the Birth

If an unusually large kid gets stuck passing through the hips, you may help gently with a careful tug on the front legs. If in the unusual instance the hind feet appear first, which you can tell because the bottoms of the hoofs will be turned upward, you should assist in case of stoppage with a gentle tug on the hind legs, since in this position amniotic fluid can get into the kid's airway if the birth goes on too long.

If a kid appears in neither the front position nor the rear position,

you can try to reposition it. After carefully cleansing your hands and the entry to the vagina, use a moment between contractions to try to press the kid that is stuck in the birth canal back into the uterus and then to position it for the normal front or rear end delivery. It is pointless to pull on the kid if the limbs are not in the proper position.

If your attempts are in vain, you should call the veterinarian. If necessary, he or she can assist the birth with medications or intervene surgically.

Warning: Birth assistance should be undertaken only by someone who has sufficient knowledge and ability. If you have any doubts, always call the veterinarian. The wrong kind of help at the birth can be torture to the animals.

Raising Kids

Maintenance

Under natural conditions the kids grow up in the herd and suckle their mothers for several months until the milk usually dries up. Generally—in contrast to sheep—there is no lasting contact between mother and kid. During the first few weeks the kids are withdrawn into a hiding place, such as a crack in the rocks or a clump of bushes, while the mother ranges quite far in the search for food. She summons them only three or four times daily with a very special bleat to come out to nurse. After this first secret phase, the kids become more venturesome and begin to explore their new world. They do this together with other kids, and under the supervision of the older goats they develop a kind of kids' school in which they gradually become quite independent of their mother and soon only seek her out to nurse.

Kids' Stable

Anyone who keeps milk goats will not wish to allow the kids to remain with their mothers for months at a time. Their natural behavior pattern facilitates raising them separately from the mother. After the kids have received their very rich milk just after birth, they can be transferred to their own nursery stable. This must be absolutely dry and free of drafts. Then the still cold-susceptible kids can tolerate a stable temperature of only 50°F (10°C) well. You can recognize a chilled kid easily by the ruffled fur on its back. If the temperature is too cold for it, place the kid in a high, open box cushioned with straw. In addition, you can hang an infrared lamp over the box for warmth, as is done for raising pigs.

During the first two weeks of life, the kids need very little room, since they mostly lie dozing. Then, however, they require increasingly more space to give free rein to their need to exercise, preferably together in a group of other kids. These little goats are grateful for an upside-down box, which they use as a climbing rock and on which they also love to lie

A newborn should be given warmth with heat lamps.

down to rest. The straw littering the kids' stable must be changed frequently, because on their diet of mainly liquid food, they urinate often and the litter quickly becomes damp.

Exercise Outdoors

Fresh air and sunlight foster health and disease resistance in the growing goats. They should have exercise in the open air whenever possible. The ideal is a special kids' pasture, where no other goats graze and that has at most been grazed until early summer the year before and at best not at all. Otherwise, the kids will be exposed to a storm of internal parasites, to which they still cannot offer sufficient resistance. If the pasture does not meet these standards, a paved run is preferable because it can be cleaned regularly.

Feeding

The newborn kid is nourished exclusively with milk, which is digested in the rennet stomach. It provides the kid with high value albumin and with B vitamins, since the kid is not yet a ruminant like the adult goat. Still, all the hereditary equipment for this is at hand. Even the eating behaviors of kids are aimed at developing their cud-chewing characteristics as uninterruptedly as possible. It pays to support this natural tendency.

Colostrum

Sufficient intake of colostrum immediately after birth is crucial for the healthy development of the kid in its first weeks of life. This milk is produced at the approach of birth and differs from ordinary milk in having a higher nutrient content and protective proteins, the so-called immunoglobulins. In contrast to human beings, the developing kid cannot be provided with these through the bloodstream of the mother during pregnancy. The kid is only able to take these immunoglobulins from the milk into its bloodstream through the intestine for a few hours after birth. Therefore, it is imperative that it ingest the colostrum as soon and as much as possible. In addition, the colostrum promotes the excretion of the meconium from the newborn kid's intestinal tract.

Nursing

If you leave the mother and her kids together during the first weeks, you should make sure that the kids are sucking properly. You may have to give a little help to the kid that is clumsily placed because of a badly shaped or very full udder. You can also separate the kids from the mother after the first nursing in order to get them used to drinking.

Drinking

The first day they get as much of the mother's milk as they can drink, on the second day only about ½ quart (0.5 L), and then, in daily increasing quantities, up to 1½ quarts (1.5 L) by the seventh day. This milk quantity should be divided into three portions during the day.

You can use a baby bottle to get the kids to drink or you can get the animals used to the pan right away. For pan drinking, you first let the kid suck on your finger. Then you lead it slowly to the dish and hold its mouth in the milk until it begins to drink by itself. The longer the kid nurses on the bottle, the more difficult it is to make the change to drinking out of a pan. With the bottle there is also the danger that the kid will take in the milk too quickly and will overload the rennet stomach. Furthermore, the milk must absolutely be at body temperature. It's best to warm it to 104°F (40°C) so that it will not get colder than 98.6°F (37°C) while it is being drunk. If you use a drinking dish, however, make sure that it is always very carefully cleaned.

The milk quantities given in the drinking plan section that follows

Two kids climbing and playing in the sun.

are quite sufficient. Don't let your-self be lured by the kid's eagerness into giving it larger quantities. This will interfere with the intake of sup-plementary plant feed and inhibit the kid's natural development into a ruminant.

Over a period of time symptoms of mineral deficiency, particularly iron deficiency, occur on a diet of milk alone. Also, an excessive milk ration can produce dangerous digestive disturbances.

Solid Food and Water

In the second week, the kids are already beginning to nibble on solid food. At this juncture, the kids

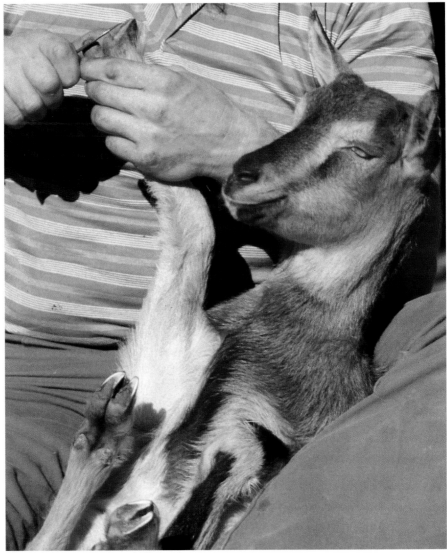

The correct way to trim a kid's hoof.

receive hay, grass fodder, and water. Fresh, clean feed must be continually available, even if in the beginning only a little of it is used. The best hay, as leafy as possible, should be reserved for the kids. A special starting fodder for lambs or calves can be used as concentrated feed; both of these are available commercially. But you can mix your own feed just as well; the following mixture has proved to be good:

Oats and barley	40%
Wheat bran	20%
Soy chips (groats)	12%
Linseed oilcake meal	25%
Mineral mixture	3%

The grains should be only coarsely ground, not as fine as meal. Oats in the form of rolled oats are ideal but unfortunately very expensive. In addition, a mineral lick is important.

The drinking water should not be ice-cold but should not be warm either, because, otherwise, small kids can't tell it from milk and can easily drink too much.

Weaning from Milk

At the age of three months, the kids are weaned. They have then a weight of about 40 pounds (18 kg), whereas at birth they weighed about 7½ pounds (3.5 kg). The kids can also be weaned earlier as long as they take in enough feed, that is, at least 14 ounces (400 g) of concentrated feed daily.

Drinking Plan

First week: Nurse from the mother; or nurse until full from the mother once, then drink three times daily; daily drinking quantities of ½ quart (0.5 L) should slowly increase to 1¾ quarts (1.5 L) of mother's milk.

Second week: Drink twice daily. Increase quantities only slowly to 2 quarts (2 L) per day.

Dehorning and Hoof Care

If you intend to have an animal dehorned, this should take place in the first week of life.

Hoofs are first trimmed at the age of six weeks. After that you must examine them at intervals of about two months and correct them by trimming if necessary. Attentive hoof care of the kid is a prerequisite for healthy legs and joints in the adult goat.

Third to eighth week: Drink twice daily, 2 quarts (2 L) per day.

From the ninth week: Drink twice daily. Slowly decrease the quantity to 1 quart (1 L) per day.

Twelfth week: Stop milk (wean).

Raising Without Mother's Milk

If a kid has taken enough colostrum, in principle it is possible to raise it without mother's milk. It is best if the kid drinks mother's milk in the first week; after that, this can be replaced with the milk of other goats. Cow's milk is also possible or a milk substitute for calves, a skim-milk powder reinforced with nutrients and hormones. In the preparation of the milk with milk substitute, the fat content should not exceed 3.5 percent.

If the colostrum is lacking—for instance, if the mother dies during the birth—the kid's chances for survival are poor unless another goat has happened to bear a kid at the same time. Therefore, it is advisable to keep a frozen supply of colostrum, which if necessary can even come from a cow.

If it should ever be needed, it should first be warmed carefully to 104°F (40°C). Then, it should be placed into a nursing bottle and given to the new kid.

Health Problems with Kids

If a kid has had colostrum early enough and in sufficient quantity, the foundation for healthy development has been laid. All the same, health problems do occur now and again.

Diarrhea

Cause

In most cases, diarrhea is a harmless digestive disturbance, induced by eating too fast, by too much or too cold milk, or by too fast a change of feed. The real danger is that serious infections can occur as a consequence of diarrhea, induced by ordinarily harmless microorganisms that are present in all healthy animals.

Signs of Illness

Liquid feces, in advanced phases, watery to foamy, indicates possible illness. The color is often yellowish but can also be gray to black and be mixed with blood. Not infrequently, kids have a bloated belly with diarrhea, which hurts them so that they arch their backs.

With infectious diarrhea there is also fever. Kids quickly waste away with persistent diarrhea.

Treatment and Prevention

Naturally, it is best to avoid the occurrence of any diarrhea at all through careful giving of milk. The early intake of solid food, which is promoted by limiting the milk portions, diminishes the risk of digestive disturbances. If diarrhea still occurs, the concentrated feed and milk are removed at once and for at least 24 hours. Instead, let the kids drink warm chamomile or black tea with charcoal or oak bark powder dissolved in it. In the majority of cases the diarrhea can be stopped this way. Afterward give them only small quantities of milk and slowly increase again to the normal fluid quantities. Water and licks should also be available during a bout of diarrhea. If the kids are already several weeks old and are eating roughage, you can quickly bring the diarrhea to a halt with the addition of pine and spruce branches or with oak leaves. It is wrong to combat diarrhea by depriving the animals of water.

Fluid and mineral loss can be compensated for by a special electrolyte solution, which can be prepared by the goat keeper:

2 teaspoons of table salt

1 teaspoon of sodium bicarbonate (drugstore)

8 tablespoons of grape sugar or honey (do not use normal cane or beet sugar!)

Dissolve these ingredients in 4 quarts (4 L) of warm water.

These proportions must be followed exactly, for a higher concentration can produce serious consequences. On the other hand, the animals can be watered with this solution in whatever quantities they will take, and it is often astonishing how quickly they recover.

Note: Continued diarrhea can soon become life threatening. If it cannot be stopped by the methods described or if it is at all bloody, you should get the veterinarian's advice. He or she will, possibly after a fecal examination and a resistance test, fight the infection with specific medications.

Worms and Coccidia

Cause

Whereas practically every goat is infested with internal parasites without exhibiting any health problems, the kids must first get used to them. Only if the burden is increased slowly can they develop resistance successfully.

Signs of Illness

If the parasite infestation is too great, the kids will display a bristly coat, pale mucous membranes, lack of appetite, or, merely, diminished growth. Diarrhea appears periodically; one recognizes such animals by the feces-smeared tail area, even if they do not quite have acute diarrhea. With coccidiosis the diarrhea may be mixed with blood.

Not seldom, the illness leads to death.

Treatment and Prevention

The veterinarian can confirm these parasites with a fecal examination and then treat with medications. Kids are wormed for the first time at the age of six to eight weeks at the earliest. Stringent hygiene measures can keep the parasites within bounds. Stable air and bedding areas must be dry, and the kids' stable should be regularly cleaned and disinfected at least once a year. Also, the hygienic measures for the kids' pasture must be carefully observed. Protect racks, troughs, and drinking water so that feed and water cannot be fouled. Sufficient roughage in the feed diminishes the risk of coccidiosis.

Enterotoxemia

Cause

With excessive milk intake and with rapid change of feed—in particular, a sharp increase in the concentrated feed portion—certain bacteria (*Clostridium*) in the intestine of the kid suddenly increase and produce a poison that can bring about sudden death.

Signs of Illness

Diarrhea, weakness, the staggers, and muscle cramps may be signs of illness. Usually particularly well-nourished kids are the ones affected. Death can occur out of the blue.

Treatment and Prevention

Call the veterinarian, but don't allow yourself to hope for a successful cure. Prevent the illness with moderate milk rations, only a gradual change of feed, and a regular ration of roughage. In problem situations, the veterinarian may try an immunizing shot.

Rickets

Cause

The ultraviolet rays contained in sunlight promote the development of vitamin D in the body. If the kids are continually kept in the stable, they do not receive these rays. The result is abnormal bone development from lack of vitamin D, especially if there are mineral deficiencies at the same time.

Signs of Illness

Difficulty walking and crooked limbs are signs of illness.

Treatment and Prevention

Rickets almost never occurs in kids that have regular outdoor exercise. If the kids are constantly kept in the stable, they need supplementary vitamin D. If you buy lamb starter feed, this already has vitamins added. Mineral feed also usually has vitamins added.

You can get vitamin preparations from the veterinarian to mix into the drinking water.

Make sure you regularly provide minerals for the kids; a lick should always be available to them. Limbs already greatly deformed can no longer be corrected by additional vitamin D.

Castration

Since the little bucks that are not going to be raised to become breeding bucks are often slaughtered before they reach sexual maturity, castration of them may not be necessary.

If an adult buck not meant to breed is to achieve a greater weight, it is advisable to have him castrated by your veterinarian at the age of one to two weeks. The buck odor can be unpleasantly noticeable in the meat of a male that has not been castrated.

Chapter Nine
Goat Products

Milk

Udder

The goat udder consists of two halves separated by a strong band of connective tissue, which bears the principal burden of the udder. The interior of each half consists of glandular vesicles, which are arranged like bunches of grapes around a central cavity, the milk cistern. From the cistern the teat canal leads through the teat to the exterior. The udder is interlaced with many blood vessels, through which the materials for the production of milk are transported to it. The milk is then secreted by the glandular vesicles into the cistern.

As the goat grows older, the udder tends to lower, sagging more and more. This can go so far that milking is made difficult, the goat is hindered in walking, and the udder is in danger of injury. Therefore, when you choose goats for breeding you must look for udders with plenty of ground clearance. Udders in which the two halves are clearly separated from each other by a cleft seldom sag even in age.

Lactation

Lactation denotes the time from the beginning of milk production after birth to the drying up of milk, usually during the subsequent pregnancy.

The daily milk output increases quickly after birth, reaching its high point in the second month and then gradually falling off. In a goat that kids yearly, the milk dries after a lactation period of 250 to 300 days. Goats that do not become pregnant for a time can display markedly longer lactation periods.

In a goat that produces 1,764 pounds (800 kg) of milk in 300 days, the highest daily production amounts to about 9 pounds (4 kg) of milk.

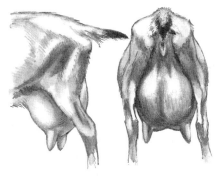

An example of a good shape. Only a roomy udder will yield much milk.

Good milk goats are distinguished not only by a high daily milk output at the beginning of the lactation period, but also because the daily milk production falls off very slowly as lactation progresses.

The young goat kidding for the first time does not immediately reach the highest production level but gradually increases up to the third and fourth kidding.

Goat's Milk

Goat's milk consists of about 88 percent water. The 12 percent of solid substances consists of fat, albumin, lactose, minerals, and vitamins. In European milk goat breeds, the nutrients are contained in these approximate average proportions: fat, 3.4 percent; albumin, 3.0 percent; lactose, 4.0 percent. In goat breeds with smaller milk production, the nutrient content is usually somewhat higher. The nutrients in the colostrum after birth are twice as high, with the albumin and fat content very much higher. By the fourth day after birth, the normal milk composition is reestablished. Though milk production falls off with progressing lactation, the nutrient content increases somewhat. Nutrients are the highest in the final milk suckled or milked out of the udder.

Quality

Goat's milk is an excellent source of nutrition, especially for small children and invalids. Therefore, there are many special, health-producing char-acteristics ascribed to it. Not all of them can be scientifically validated.

It may be that the oft-mentioned easy digestibility of goat's milk is due to the fact that the fat is dispersed differently and is in finer particles than in cow's milk. It is certain that, for children who are allergic to cow's milk, the change to goat's milk can help, since the protein is somewhat differently composed from that of cow's milk. Unfortunately, there are children who are allergic to both kinds of protein.

Color and Taste

Goat's milk, and thus also goat butter, is completely white, since in contrast to cow's milk it contains no carotene, a precursor of vitamin A. On the other hand, the milk and butter contain much more vitamin A. Freshly milked, goat's milk tastes little different from cow's milk. The typical, somewhat strong goat's-milk taste develops a little later. Highly prized in goat cheese, it is not so popular in milk for drinking, especially if, in addition, it is tainted by the dirt and odor of the stable. Clean udders and milk pails are thus especially important.

Unavoidably, any milk produced by milking contains a certain amount of dirt and bacteria. At normal temperatures, these multiply quickly and produce a change, primarily souring.

Milking

Goats are easier to milk than sheep and cows, since a major portion of the milk is already in the udder cistern, from which it is easily milked. The milk in the glandular vesicles will be freed by milking when they are contracted under the direction of a hormone that is released in reaction to the manipulation of the udder.

There are two kinds of milking: hand milking and machine milking.

Hand Milking

Here we distinguish between two methods, the *fist* and the *knuckles*. The better and more considerate method is the *fist*. In this method the thumb and forefinger close the teat tightly at the udder, while the middle, ring, and little finger press the milk out of the teat. This way the hand itself does not move up and down and does not pull on the udder. If the teat is quite short, the milk is pressed out with two fingers or even with one.

If the goat has very short teats, you can also use the *knuckle* method. In this one, the thumb is bent forward and the base of the teat is pressed against the thumb knuckle with the forefinger. Thus the udder-teat passage is closed and the milk is pressed out of the teat canal with the middle finger.

If you are milking goats from the right side, the left hand grasps the right teat and the right hand grasps the left teat of the goat. When the milk flow decreases, continue to milk with the right hand and then stroke out the udder with the left hand from top to bottom. In many places, goats are also milked from behind.

Milking by hand (fist milking)

In fist milking, the teat canal is first closed off from the cistern with the thumb and forefinger.

Then the other fingers one after the other, press the milk out of the teat canal.

Hard grasping will injure the delicate skin in the interior of the udder.

This diagram shows how to milk a goat by hand.

Machine Milking

A milking machine for goats is similar in construction to one for cows, except that of course it has only two teat cups. It imitates the suckling kid and draws the milk from the udder by means of a vacuum in a regular alternation between sucking and resting phases. The ratio of sucking to resting phases should be

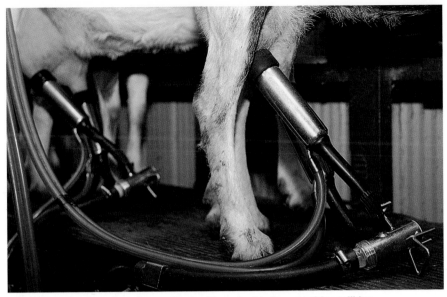

Milking suction cups have been attached in order to allow machine milking.

about 1:1 to 2:1, with the recommended sucking-resting cycles at 70 to 90 per minute, and the sucking vacuum at 40 to 44 kPa. Failure to maintain these technical specifications precisely will result in serious injuries to the udder.

With machine milking you must also see to it that the machine is quickly detached from the udder as soon as the milk flow comes to an end, because blind milking injures the udder tissue and promotes udder inflammation. When you see through the transparent top of the teat cup that the milk flow is diminishing, stroke out the udder with the left hand as in hand milking and then with the right hand draw the milking equipment toward the front feet. If the udder is limp and empty, close

the vacuum valve and remove the milking apparatus. As a control, a bit more can still be milked by hand. Since the amount of work of cleaning, disinfecting, and servicing milking equipment is high, its use makes sense economically only with a herd of about 25 milk goats or larger. If the primary consideration is to lighten the work of milking, using a milking machine with even smaller herds is reasonable. There are small portable machines available for this.

Foremilking

Since the first two to three streams of milk contain many germs, you should milk these out of each teat into a foremilk container. This has a black coating that allows you to examine the foremilk carefully to

Goats lined up for the milking machine.

detect the early signs of inflammation, such as coloration and flakes.

After foremilking, the udder is wiped dry, preferably with a paper towel used only once. Damp udder cloths transfer bacteria from goat to goat. After that, begin milking. In hand milking, the udder is carefully and uninterruptedly milked empty, but not with force, until the last drops are squeezed out.

Dipping

Dipping is recommended to inhibit the bacteria of udder inflammation, which mainly enter the teat canal after the extraction of the milk. Dip or plunge the teats immediately after milking, especially after machine milking, into a container with a spe-

cial iodine disinfectant solution. Goats that are known to have udder inflammation should always be milked last.

Milking Stand

Your work will be made easier with a milking stand on which you can milk the goats cleanly and comfortably without bending. If only one goat is to be milked at a time, a simple wooden platform with a height of about 19½ to 31 inches (50 to 80 cm) is enough; the goat can jump up on this for milking, possibly lured by some concentrated feed in a trough. Don't tie several goats there together. On larger milking stands, several goats can be milked by machine at the same time.

Uses of Milk

Storage

After milking, you should strain the milk as quickly as possible through a cotton filter. Straining cloths are not suitable, since they must be boiled after each use. Paper coffee filters are a makeshift alternative, because they allow the milk to drain through only very slowly.

Next, the milk must be stored in a cold place—small quantities in a refrigerator, larger quantities in a cooling can or a cooling tank. You can also store milk in a cool cellar for about a day or place the milk can in a trough through which cold water flows. For longer storage, the best is a container of stainless steel, which is the easiest to clean and to disinfect.

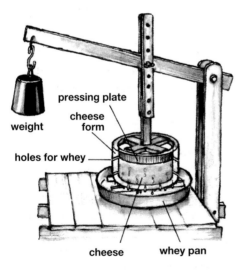

weight
pressing plate
cheese form
holes for whey
cheese
whey pan

An example of a custom-made cheese press for the production of hard cheese.

Sour Milk and Yogurt

If you store fresh goat's milk at room temperature, it thickens and sours by itself. It works even better if you inoculate the fresh milk with a bit of already soured milk. To make yogurt, you must inoculate the fresh milk with yogurt culture and keep it warm for 12 hours at exactly 104°F (40°C). A special electric yogurt maker is good for this. You can buy yogurt culture or simply use a tablespoon of prepared yogurt as culture for a glass of fresh milk. Yogurt from goat's milk is more liquid than yogurt made from cow's milk.

Cheese

Goat cheese is the most important product of goat's milk; because of its special aroma and its consistency it is highly prized as a delicacy. But the preparation of cheese is also an opportunity to conserve the nutrients in the fresh milk, which is otherwise easily spoiled. There are countless different varieties of goat cheese all over the world, of which most are produced by the following basic steps:
• souring
• curdling with rennet
• separating the cheese mass from the whey
• salting and drying
• ripening.

Prerequisites for successful cheese making are painstaking cleanliness and as precise as possible a control of temperature. Rinse all equipment and containers after using, first with warm, not hot, water. Then wash the milk utensils in a combined cleaning and disinfectant solution and dry them in the air, preferably in the sun. Once weekly, wash the equipment in a vinegar solution or with an acidic cleaning material. All cloths must first be carefully cleaned and then boiled.

The following recipe contains all the basic steps of cheese making. Don't let yourself be discouraged if you have failures. Soon you will succeed with this cheese and then can try other cheese types, which are mostly only variations on this basic principle.

• For equipment, you need a pail for the milk, an accurate fluid thermometer 68° to 158°F (20° to 70°C), a large knife, pierced cheese molds, cheese matting, and cheesecloth. The cheese-making room should be at room temperature.

• Use milk that is no more than 24 hours old. Also, if you are being self-sufficient, you should make cheese from at least 5 to 10 quarts (5 to 10 L), since with smaller quantities the milk and the cheese mass cool too quickly for the culture to act.

Souring

Heat the milk to a temperature of 95°F (35°C). Then add yogurt or sour milk or a mixture of both (about ¼ quart per 10½ quarts [¼ L per 10 L] milk) to start the souring process. You can also use a specially formulated cheese culture or whey from the last cheese. Let the whole thing stand for 15 minutes.

Pasteurizing

If you are producing cheese for sale, it is advisable to pasteurize the milk for hygienic reasons and thus also to fulfill the legal requirements. Since the brief heating method for pasteurizing is almost impossible to do precisely with a normal-sized herd, the milk can also be pasteurized by extended heating over 30 minutes at 143.6° to 149°F (62° to 65°C). However, this method is not recognized legally everywhere as adequate for food. Under no circumstances should the milk boil, or its capability of being made into cheese will be destroyed by alteration of the protein structure. In the production of hard cheese, the pasteurization precautions are not necessary: the bacteria die out during the long aging process.

Curdling with Rennet

Now you coagulate the milk, using rennet, an enzyme from the stomach of calves. Rennet comes in liquid form or as tablets; use it according to the instructions of the producer. With liquid rennet you achieve the exact dose by using a pipette, since you need only 10 to 20 drops of rennet for 10 quarts (10 L) of milk. The milk should be at a temperature of 89.6°F (32°C) for curdling. You can stir the rennet quickly and thoroughly into the milk, or you can do it the other way around and put the rennet into an empty container and add the milk to it. The milk and the rennet are especially well mixed this way.

To curdle, let the milk stand undisturbed and uncovered until, after several hours, it has become firm and gelatinous.

Breaking

In the next step, the cheese is "broken." With the knife, cut the gelatin into squares about 1½ by 1½ inches (4 cm by 4 cm) and let the liquid whey run out. After 30 to 60 minutes, pour off a portion of the drained-out whey, halve the squares, and let the whey drain again. Then cut up the pieces of cheese again, until the remaining crumbs have an edge length of 0.39 inches (1 cm).

Draining and Pressing

Curds have developed from the draining off of the whey from the cheese particles. Scoop these curds into a cheesecloth or simply into a muslin napkin, hang up this cheese mass like a sack, and let the whey drip out entirely. You can use the curds now as fresh cheese with herbs and garlic.

If you want to go further, pack the dried crumbs into a perforated cheese mold of plastic, aluminum, wood, or terra-cotta and set it aside at room temperature for more whey to come out.

To help along the release of the whey even more, the developing cheese can also be pressed in these molds. Lay a form-fitting cover on the cheese and press with a weight, or place the cheese in a cheese press. It's a good idea to line the form with a piece of cheesecloth before you start, to make turning the finished cheese out of the form easier. The more whey that is expressed, the firmer the cheese will be.

Salting and Drying

After 24 to 36 hours, the cheese is taken out of the mold and salted. To do this, you can place it for two to three hours in a 16 to 18 percent solution of table salt. Less effort but more fingertip feeling and experience is required for dry salting. Cover the cheese thinly but as closely as possible with a coating of salt, as if one grain lay close against the next. Place the salted cheese on the cheese matting and dry it for two days in an airy room or out-of-doors. To be sure the outside of the cheese dries evenly, you must turn the cheese regularly.

Ripening

To ripen the cheese place it in a damp, coot cellar. Keep checking it and turning it so that it doesn't get moldy.

After four to seven days, the cheese is ready. It is a mild cheese that doesn't stay fresh for very long, but you can preserve it for a longer time if you lay it in olive oil. Add some thyme, rosemary, a few peppercorns, juniper berries, garlic, and pepperoni to the oil; this promotes that fine spicy aroma of goat cheese.

You can vary this basic recipe by
- adding more or less rennet
- cutting the cheese coarser or finer

- warming the cut cheese slightly
- letting it dry more or less
- pressing it more or less
- drying it for a shorter or longer time.

You will soon advance in the art of cheese making and can produce the cheese you like best or a whole variety.

Using the Whey

Whey, the by-product, primarily contains lactose, lactic acid, and some albumin. It can be fed to pigs, but it is also prized as a nutritious drink. The albumin remaining in it can be precipitated out of the soured whey by boiling and is then pressed through a sieve. Such a cooked cheese can also be produced from fresh milk, which is brought to a boil while being stirred. When it is boiling, add some vinegar, vinegar essence, or lemon juice to form cheese flakes. Wrap these in a cheesecloth and let the whey run off. Since this cooked cheese has little flavor of its own, salt and season it according to your taste.

Butter

Goat's milk doesn't form cream as readily as cow's milk. Therefore, it is advisable to separate the cream from the milk with a centrifuge and churn it to butter. There are centrifuges and butter churns that are operated by hand for small quantities. As soon as the butter lumps are about the size of a pea, the buttermilk is drawn off. Then the butter must be washed and kneaded several times in cold water until the water runs clear, that is, until all the buttermilk is washed out; otherwise, the butter will go bad quickly. It will keep even better with the addition of table salt.

Goat butter is also a popular base for salves.

Meat

Meat Yield

Even if you don't wish to keep goats for meat, there will still be young animals born that you do not need to raise, or there will be adult animals that are no longer necessary, for one reason or another. Insofar as you are not against the killing of animals in principle and you enjoy eating meat, you will need to use the meat of these animals as a by-product of your goat keeping. But it is also possible that meat is to be the chief product. If so, you will mainly slaughter kids at the age of eight to ten weeks at a weight of 22 to 26 pounds (10 to 12 kg), or sell them for slaughter at that age and weight. Kid's meat is considered a delicacy by gourmets; at Easter, especially, there is great demand for it. On the average, after skinning and removal of the head, tail, hoofs, and entrails, a kid carcass weighs 50 percent of the original living weight. Of this carcass about 70 percent is meat.

Castrated bucks slaughtered at the age of one to two years produce tasty roasting meat.

The meat of older goats, because it is dry, is most suited to the pro-

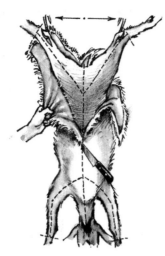

Once a goat is skinned, its carcass should be hung as shown in the diagram.

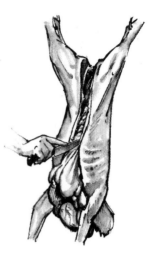

When a carcass is drawn, the belly and chest cavity are opened from the anal area to the breastbone with a single cut.

duction of hard sausage when mixed with fattier pork. The lower quantity of fat is typical of the meat of younger as well as older goats.

Slaughtering

All animals for slaughter, even kids under three months, must be inspected before and after slaughtering by the meat inspector as provided by regulations. The inspector then passes the meat for use.

To arrange for a kid or full-grown goat to be slaughtered, contact the local slaughterhouse.

Skinning

The throat is cut and the arteries opened to drain the blood. The animal is then hung up by the spread hind legs. The skin on the inside of the back legs is cut up to the belly, loosened around the rear hoofs with

a round cut, and pulled off. In many places the skin will come free merely with pulling, but sometimes it must be helped with the knife. This is continued to the belly and insides of the front legs. Tail, testicles, udder, head, and hoofs are then cut off.

In the skinning of sexually mature bucks, the sexual odor can very easily be transmitted to the meat from the skin. It is therefore better to castrate bucks several weeks before slaughtering so that this odor is gone. But, in principle, it is possible to slaughter uncastrated bucks with very clean and careful skinning so that the meat retains little or no buck odor.

After the skin is off, the abdominal cavity is opened with a smooth cut from anus to breastbone. Then the entrails, liver, and gallbladder are carefully removed.

Hanging

The carcass, dirtied with hair, blood, and stomach and intestinal contents, is washed and hung to age for several days in a cool place. The flesh of newly slaughtered animals is still tough and has little flavor, but the longer the meat hangs, the more tender it becomes. For storage of longer than three days, a cold-storage room is required. For cutting up, divide according to the anatomy: legs, back, neck, ribs. It is also highly advisable to entrust the making of hard sausage to an expert, since durability is guaranteed only when the correct procedure is followed very precisely.

Other Products

Skin

Goatskin is a valuable raw product for making expensive grained and sueded leathers. Demand and price are considerable. However, the manufacturing industry buys only large lots, so that single skins are practically unsalable. You can give these to a dresser and then work them yourself into purses and such or simply use them for decoration. For use as fur, only the skins of very young kids are suitable, because their coat is still very soft, supple, and shining.

If you cannot have the skin tanned right away, it must be carefully prepared for storage. This is done by salting or drying. At first, carefully clean off the remains of flesh without injuring the skin. Then

Many people raise goats for their meat.

strew the skin side with salt. You can also stretch the skin to dry on a frame, or stretch and nail it to a large board, and preserve it this way until you can take it to the dresser.

Mohair

Angora goats are shorn twice a year, as a rule, with a total shearing yield of about 11 pounds (5 kg) raw weight. This hair is washed like sheep's wool and manufactured further, resulting in the soft but hard-wearing mohair. Since the textile industry needs large lots—if possible, sorted as to quality—you must take care of the manufacture yourself if you are keeping only a small angora herd.

Cashmere

Cashmere is the underhair of goats that is shed with the change of hair in the spring. Especially prized is that of Kashmir goats in the high mountains of northern India and central Asia, where cashmere is gathered by combing it out. It is a very thin fiber, which is used for the finest knitwear and fabric. But, frequently, the goats of the breeds kept in Europe and America also display a remarkable development of underhair in winter, especially if they are kept under cold conditions. If you have some experience in the processing of wool, you should try to collect the shed underhair in the spring and process it.

Manure

Goat manure is a valuable fertilizer, especially if it originates from an open stable from an intimate mixture of dung and urine. It is suitable for fertilizing in the garden and farm fields as well as in pastures.

The Economics of Goat Keeping

If you are keeping goats primarily so that you can be self-sufficient, you are less interested in the financial gain, although you must certainly be sure that your expense in money and work earns an appropriate return. The value of this return does not consist only of a sum of money, however, since the self-sufficient farmer considers it important to be the producer himself. Nevertheless, if you are trying to make money from goat husbandry, it is not enough in itself to aim for a high output with good production technology. The chief problem in having an economically successful goat farm is the marketing. Goat products are certainly in demand and well paid for, as the supply is small, but eventually this will not be reason enough. With an increase in the supply, these prices may possibly not hold.

There is no established marketing organization you can join to facilitate marketing goat products. In most instances, you must, yourself, market the products directly to the consumer. On the one hand, this means more work; on the other, you thereby avoid the middleman, a solution that is advantageous to both seller and buyer and promotes the confidence of the consumer in the producer.

If you want to increase your goat holdings, it makes sense to do so in small steps, so that you can develop an appropriate clientele at the same time. Many farmers, however, look for more than material profit in their goat operations and take pleasure in the cheerful nature of their goats.

Chapter Ten

Goat Breeds of the World

The Ancestry of the Domestic Goat

In the zoological classification of the animal kingdom, the goat belongs to the cloven-hoofed, ruminant family of the Bovidae, the horned ones, to which sheep, cattle, and gazelles also belong, but not deer. Along with the sheep and other relatives such as the musk ox and the chamois, they constitute a subfamily in which four wild goat species make up the genus of the goat, *Capra*.

Capra ibex: The ibex, including the subspecies of the mountain goat and the Nubian ibex of the mountains around the Red Sea and of turs in the Caucasus, which are sometimes considered the same.

Capra pyrenaica: The Spanish ibex.

Capra hircus: The bezoar goat in the mountains of western Asia from the Greek islands to the Himalayas.

Capra falconieri: The markhor in Afghanistan and Pakistan, which is especially striking because of its twisted curled horns, whereas the other wild goat species have saber-shaped horns.

All these wild goat species are still extant today. The existence of the Nubian ibex is threatened, unfortunately, whereas the existence of the mountain goat is protected by stringent conservation regulations. The numbers of wild goats in Greece is dwindling, to be sure, but they are protected in a national park in Crete.

In many regions in Asia, wild goats are heavily hunted and are in some danger of extermination.

Wild goats live in all mountainous places. Their body build and their lifestyle are extraordinarily well adapted to this environment, and many characteristics of our domestic goats are a legacy of this adaptation. It is certain that the domestic goat stems primarily from the bezoar goat, and only some domestic goat breeds in central Asia appear also to have the markhor as an ancestor.

Drawings from ancient Egypt show that the Nubian ibex was held in captivity there. But it was not actually domesticated.

Clearly, the alpine ibex does not belong to the ancestors of the domestic goat, not even in the modern domesticated alpine breeds.

humans. Archeological finds in regions of Iran, the Fertile Crescent, Anatolia, and Palestine indicate that goats were domesticated as early as 7000 B.C. From this center of domestication, the goat spread over Asia, Africa, and Europe. In the new world, the domestic goat arrived with the European settlers.

Today, worldwide, there are some 480 million domestic goats, about 95 percent of them in the developing countries. Particularly numerous goat stocks are found in Africa and the Near East, where there is a goat for every three inhabitants, whereas in the developed countries on the average there is one goat for every 50 inhabitants. In the United States there exists a stock of 3 to 4 million goats—with Texas leading in angora and meat goats, and California leading in dairy goats.

Certainly in earlier days, when ibex were much more numerous in the Alps, it did occasionally happen that goats grazing in mountain pastures were covered by ibex. But even if the resulting crossed animals went on to breed, the inheritance of the ibex was quickly lost again.

Mating of goats with chamois does not occur and would not be fruitful.

The Distribution of the Domestic Goat

After the dog, the goat is probably the animal most domesticated by

Goat Keeping All over the World

There are a variety of forms of goat keeping, depending on the circumstances of the particular goat keeper; the main types are summarized in the following overview.

Family Holdings

The family holding is a small holding of a few goats or even of a single animal for the purpose of self-

sufficiency, particularly for milk, and this is the form in which most goats are kept all over the world. The goats are fed with household scraps and on otherwise unused areas—for example, the edges of roads—are tied in fields, or are herded, mostly by children or old people. Or food is collected and given to an animal that is tied or is in a stable. This form of maintenance is found not only with farm families or landless day workers and hand workers in towns, but also with city dwellers too, who must also buy the feed.

In Germany, the goat has thus earned the name "mountaineer's cow" or "railroader's cow," for in time of need, goat keeping has eased the survival of more than a few families, if indeed it has not actually made survival possible.

Sometimes a family will sell the milk from its cow, and keep goats for the family's own milk needs. This was the practice in many small farming regions in southern Germany until not too long ago: All the cow's milk was sold to the milk processing plant, while the family itself drank goat's milk. In the Swiss mountains today, goats still serve as the milk supply in the summer when the cows are up in the mountain meadows. There, it is common practice to gather the village goats together in a herd in the morning, take them to pasture on the mountain, and drive them back again to the village in the evening for milking. Since it is diffi-

cult to find herders for this strenuous herding work, there are fewer and fewer of these "home herds," as they are called.

Pets

With growing prosperity as well as with increasing specialization in agriculture, family goat keeping in industrialized countries either is disappearing or is converted into pet keeping. In this case, the primary consideration is not practicality but the pleasure in dealing with the animals. The unusual appearance of the goat then takes on a special significance; this expresses itself in pedigreed goat breeding, which is particularly popular in Great Britain and the United States. In recent years the idea of self-sufficiency has again become important to goat fanciers, even without economic necessity. People want to know where their food has come from, and enjoy being able to eat food they have produced themselves. Economy of production is thus of less importance.

Intensive Husbandry

The intensive holding is aimed at market production. Milk production is the principal goal; intensive husbandry of meat goats is not widespread. In this form, the herd size is usually between 50 and 250 milk goats, depending on the available feeding area and the work force. The type of feeding ranges from herding to stable feeding with a high ration of concentrated feed. In France, for example, this is the most prevalent form of holding, whereas in the United States at this writing there are very few goat farms of this kind and most meat goats are reared on pasture.

Goat Keeping and Farming

When herds of goats are maintained in one place in combination with farming, the goats are usually kept with other animals—cows and especially sheep. Between seeding and harvest, they will be grazed on fallow land. Afterward they are pastured on the harvested fields and will also be fed with straw and whatever remains after threshing. The milk is usually used as well as the meat, though the latter is less prevalent. This type of husbandry is found in the farming areas of the drier tropics and subtropics, including the Mediterranean area.

Roaming

In developing countries, the goats—together with sheep, poultry, and swine—are allowed to roam in the area of human habitation, with almost no expenditure made for them. They are largely left to themselves and roam together seeking fodder, principally garbage. They furnish no regular contribution to the nourishment of the family and are only slaughtered for special occasions or, still more important, sold when ready money is required. Even if their contribution to the total income is small because of the small number of animals per family, the share of the cash receipt can still be very high.

Nomadic Grazing Economy

In the more or less defined nomadic grazing economy, the goats are kept in large herds. Partial nomadic husbandry is marked by a seasonal change between tilled field areas and purely pasture areas, between winter and summer pastures, between valley and mountain pastures. This type of husbandry is mainly found in the Mediterranean, in Asia Minor, and in the Middle East, but also in the dry areas of Africa and Latin America. Meat production is usually more important than milk production in this type of goat keeping.

Entirely nomadic management is limited to dry regions, where the thorny vegetation of the semidesert and desert can be used only by

This herd of Toggenburgs and Alpines shares a pasture.

goats or camels. The milk of these goats serves as a food supply for the nomads; animals are also sold for meat.

Ranch Husbandry

Ranching of Angora goats serves the production of mohair. This type of husbandry is primarily found in South Africa and in the southwestern United States, where extensive brushy plains do not permit profitable cattle or sheep raising. Angora goats, on the other hand, are able to use the protein-rich foliage. The pastures are fenced, and the large herds are supervised by mounted herdsmen.

Goats are distributed in practically all climatic regions of the world. A wide variety of breeds have been developed to suit the different environmental requirements and purposes. Raising goats on farms for meat production is common in the southern United States where forages are abudent.

European/American Goat Breeds

Many of the goat breeds that are kept for milk production in Europe and North America either descend directly from the goats of the Swiss mountains or have arisen from a crossing of local breeds with Swiss goats.

Two breeds are particularly important:

1. *Saanen goats,* so called from their place of origin in the Saanen

A small herd of Angoras are kept for fiber production on a ranch.

valley in the Bern Canton in Switzerland. This name is used all over the world for a white, usually hornless goat with a good milk output. (White, incidentally, is dominant over other colors.) Generally, the goats of the Saanen groups are described simply as "white goats," as, for example, the *Nederlandse Witte Geit* in The Netherlands, the *Alba de Banat* in Rumania, or the *white Edelzeige* in Germany.

2. *Alpine goats*, so-called in English- and Romance-language areas, are mostly fawn colored, although there are also black and variegated animals. They are similar to the Saanen goats in form and in milk production but are considered more robust. The alpine goats are chiefly descended from the Swiss chamois-colored goat.

German Goat Breeds

The two German goat breeds are the *white Edelziege* and the *colored*

Edelziege. The white Edelziege stems from the regional breeds through the repression of color in crossbreeding, primarily with Saanen goats, but partly also with Appenzeller goats, which are similar to Saanen goats but have longer hair. They are, as their name suggests, pure white, but often they have a soft reddish or yellowish color on the neck and also on the back. The coat is short and smooth, but it can also be longer on the neck and the back and thighs. The colored Edelziege corresponds to the alpine type. In contrast to the white Edelziege the old regional breeds were not suppressed so completely; their relationship to the different color types is always discernible. The coat of the colored Edelziege is basically brown. Darkly colored goats with black bellies and black legs are reminiscent of the former *Frankish goat* and of the *Erzgebirg goat*.

The inheritance of the former *Black Forest goat* and the *Harz goat* shows itself in an allover light color and a very light belly, which makes the legs appear black. All of these color varieties have a black streak on the back (eel-backed). This is absent in those goats that still exhibit the colors of the *Thüringer-Wald goats*. Especially striking among these goats are the color types with two light stripes that frame the face. This marking is characteristic for the *Toggenburg goats* from Switzerland, which in Thüringia have been used for the improvement of the local breed; for this reason the Thüringer-Wald goat has also been described as the German Toggenburg. The Toggenburg, which has been bred pure for over 300 years, has become very popular in the United States and England. Four inches (10 cm) shorter than the Saanen, it is also extremely affectionate.

Besides the already-mentioned breeds of Saanen, chamois-colored mountain goats, Toggenburg, and Appenzeller goats—the first three of which, especially, have achieved international importance—there are still other goat breeds of regional importance in Switzerland.

1. The Swiss *Bündner Strahlen-ziege* is black with white markings. It is an especially good walker, since in summer the flocks have to walk a long way and overcome great differences in altitude daily.

2. The Swiss *Nera Vercasca* has a tough black coat and must be particularly robust to be able to withstand the great temperature

One of the authors with a white Saanen.

extremes that frequently occur in the Tessiner Alps.

3. The *Welsh black-necked goat* has long hair, which is black at the front half of the body and white at the rear. These goats are kept mainly as meat animals, and their supply has become very small.

4. The *Golden Guernsey* is a popular English breed from the Channel Isles.

5. The *La Mancha,* developed in California from Spanish, Swiss, and Nubian stock, is known for its adaptability and good winter production.

This fully grown Alpine enjoys a quiet afternoon in a field.

This La Mancha seems interested in the photographer.

Non-European Goat Breeds

The great variety of goats in the tropics and subtropics are described below by some typical breeds that have also gained a measure of popularity in temperate climates.

1. The *Anglo-Nubian goat* was bred in Great Britain and from the Nubian goats of Egypt. Characteristic are their ram's head and hanging ears. The Anglo-Nubian goat has become extremely popular in the United States and Canada.

2. The *Pygmy* or *West African dwarf goat* has especially short legs on a relatively large torso and has a broad head. In the forest districts of West and Central Africa, it is perhaps the most important domestic animal. It is very prolific but is used only for meat, since the milk production is small and is only enough for nourishing kids. This dwarf goat is frequently encountered in zoos and

The Pygmy stands near a fence in a wooded area.

This colored German Edelziege relaxes in a pasture.

A Saanen doe and Toggenburg buck welcome each other's company.

Shami, or Damascus, goats inside a pen.

among hobby raisers in Europe and North America.

3. The *Boer goat* comes from South Africa and since the beginning of this century has been raised for meat production. Today these goats are among the few breeds specifically designated as meat breeds. Castrated mate goats can weigh up to 220 pounds (100 kg). There can be many different colors, but the breeders strive for white with red-brown neck and head. Further marks of distinction are the large hanging ears.

4. The *Kiko goat* comes from New Zealand and is large framed, generally white (although many Kikos carry genes for color), with a coat that ranges from slick in summer to flowing when run in mountain country in winter. The primary characteristic of the Kiko goat is its hardiness and its ability to achieve substantial weight gains when run under natural conditions without supplementary feeding. In New Zealand it has been called the "go anywhere, eat anything" goat, signifying its ability to thrive under less-than-ideal conditions.

Mature males display substantial characteristic horns and are of a bold disposition. Mature females are ample, feminine, and generally have good udder placement and attachment. The Kiko is claimed as a con-

A group of Kikos and Boers near their shelter.

sumate grazer and will range extensively when run in open country. The Kiko is not affected by substantial climatic variation and is equally at home in subalpine mountain country and arid brushland.

Perhaps the defining characteristic of the breed is the rate of growth. The kids are born of average size but with considerable vigor. From birth to weaning the Kiko displays a rate of growth at least equivalent to any other purpose-bred meat goat breed, but this is claimed to be achieved without the management and feed inputs generally required for satisfactory meat production.

5. The *Angora goat* stems from the highlands of Anatolia in Turkey; its name is derived from the city of Ankara. This medium-sized goat has a pure white curly coat, which is shorn to produce mohair. Besides Turkey, the Angora goat is today found primarily in South Africa and Texas. In England, France, and Germany there are some examples of Angora breeding, but the procuring of breeding animals from the traditional breeding areas is at least difficult, if not impossible, because of veterinary regulations.

6. The *Shami* or *Damascus goat* in the Near East is a large goat with good milk production. Characteristic are the ram's heads and hanging ears.

7. The *Sahara goats* are particularly well suited to their environment. This fact shows in their extraordinarily long legs, which enable the nomadic herdsmen to drive the herds

This Angora buck displays its full coat.

This Boer buck is chained to a log so that he cannot get lost.

This Welsh black-necked goat looks after her young.

across wide stretches of sandy desert to the scanty pastures and the meager watering places.

Resources

Associations

American Boer Goat Association
1207 S. Bryant Boulevard, Suite C
San Angelo, TX 76903
www.abga.org

American Dairy Goat Association
P.O. Box 865
Spindale, NC 28160
www.adga.org

American Kiko Goat Association
3663 Wayne Brayant Road
Louiseville, TN 37777
www.kikogoat.com

American Meat Goat Association
P.O. Box 676
Sonora, TX 76950
www.meatgoats.com

Canadian Goat Society
2417 Holly Lane
Ottawa, Ontario K1V 0M7
Canada
www.goats.ca/

Goat Breeders Society of Australia
P.O. Box 4317 G.P.O.
Sydney 2001, New South Wales
Australia

International Boer Goat Association
P.O. Box 1045
Whitewright, TX 75491
www.intlboergoat.org

The British Goat Society
34-36 Forestreet
Bovey Tracey
Devon TQ13 9AD
England
www.allgoats.com

Suppliers of Equipment and Books

Caprine Supply
P.O. Box Y
125 East Second Street
DeSoto, KS 66018
www.caprinesupply.com

Hoegger Supply Co.
P.O. Box 331
Fayetteville, GA 30214
www.hoeggergoatsupply.com

Premier 1
2031 300th Street
Washington, IA 52353
www.premier1supplies.com

Self-Sufficiency Supplies Ltd.
Priory Road
Wells, Somerset
England

Sydell Inc.
46935 SD Highway 50
Burbank, SD 57010
www.sydell.com

Magazines
Dairy Goat Guide (monthly)
Highway 19 East
Waterloo, WI 53594

Dairy Goat Journal (monthly)
145 Industrial Drive
Medford, WI 54451
www.dairygoatjournal.com

United Caprine News
    (monthly newsletter)
P.O. Box 328
Crowley, TX 76036
www.unitedcaprinenews.com

A Nubian doe looking for other does to congregate with.

Books
Belanger, Jerry. *Raising Milk Goats the Modern Way.* Pownal, VT: Storey Publishing, 1990.

Coleby, Pat. *Natural Goat Care.* Austin, TX: Acres, 2001.

Matthews, John. *Diseases of the Goat,* Second Edition. New York: Blackwell Publishing, 1999.

Mionczynski, John. *The Pack Goat.* Boulder, CO: Pruett Publishing Company, 1992.

Pugh, D. G. *Sheep and Goat Medicine.* Philadelphia, PA: W. B. Saunders, 2002.

Smith, Mary C. and David M. Sherman. *Goat Medicine.* Pennsylvania, PA: Lea & Febiger, 1994.

Index